MAKING THE MOST OF YOUR
PRESSURE COOKER

MAKING THE MOST OF YOUR
PRESSURE COOKER

HOW TO CREATE DELICIOUS, HEALTHY MEALS IN DOUBLE QUICK TIME

Carolyn Humphries

A HOW TO BOOK

ROBINSON

ROBINSON

First published in Great Britain in 2013 by Spring Hill,
an imprint of How To Books Ltd

This edition published in 2015 by Robinson

1 3 5 7 9 10 8 6 4 2

A CIP catalogue record for this book is available from the British Library.

ISBN: 978-1-90897-405-1

Produced for How To Books by Deer Park Productions, Tavistock, Devon
Designed and typeset by Mousemat Design Ltd
Illustrations by Verity Thompson: www.sketchy.org.uk
Printed and bound in Great Britain by Bell & Bain Ltd, Glasgow

Robinson
An imprint of
Little, Brown Book Group
Carmelite House
50 Victoria Embankment
London EC4Y 0DZ

An Hachette UK Company
www.hachette.co.uk

www.littlebrown.co.uk

NOTE: The material contained in this book is set out in good faith for general guidance and
no liability can be accepted for loss or expense incurred as a result of relying in particular
circumstances on statements made in the book. Laws and regulations are complex and liable
to change, and readers should check the current position with relevant authorities before
making personal arrangements.

How To Books are published by Robinson, an imprint of Little, Brown Book Group.
We welcome proposals from authors who have first-hand experience of their subjects.
Please set out the aims of your book, its target market and its suggested contents in an email to
Nikki.Read@howtobooks.co.uk

Contents

Introduction

In this fast-moving society we live in, no-one seems to have the time to cook from scratch for their everyday meals or, when they do, they want something that's incredibly quick to make.

Now for many people that means chucking a piece of expensive, tender meat in a pan and serving it with a salad or, at most, cooking some pasta and a simple sauce. But we can do so much better than that!

Using a pressure cooker is the way to get food fast – but not just 'fast food'! With this device, you can serve real, healthy meals for yourself and your family in a fraction of the usual time.

A pressure cooker can cut the cooking time of most foods so drastically that – just for instance – you could have a delicious hearty stew, using a cheaper cut of meat and lots of veggies, in just 20 minutes (instead of two hours cooked conventionally). That also means that, because it's quick, it saves you masses of fuel so is economical and eco-friendly into the bargain.

Plus there are other advantages, too. The food is either steamed or cooked quickly in its own juices, making sure it retains loads of valuable nutrients that promote the health of you and your family. And as the pressure cooker is a sealed container, it doesn't fug-up the kitchen nor does it permeate the house with strong odours, as most of them are contained in the cooker. The benefits just keep on piling up!

Pressure cooking is also very versatile – you probably expected to find casseroles, soups and stews in this book, but preserves, pâtés, bread, cakes, poached fish, risottos and pasta? I think you'll be surprised by the range of dishes you can cook in the pressure cooker! And that's not to mention some of the most divine desserts you can think of, like chocolate pudding with a built-in chocolate sauce or the classic crème caramel.

In *Making the Most of your Pressure Cooker*, you'll discover exactly that: how to get the best out of your pressure cooker, making it work for you to make your life easier, your cooking less stressful, and the results on the plate more varied, healthier and more delicious.

Once you've tried a few of the recipes, you'll soon begin to understand how it can become the best friend you have in your kitchen and how it can be used, on its own or in conjunction with other cooking methods, to make mouth-watering meals in record time!

The recipes in this book are based on a large 6 litre pressure cooker.

Most pressure cookers cook at one of two pressures but some have three. For the purposes of this book, I have used High pressure (12–15lb depending on your cooker) and Low pressure (5–7lb).

I used a Prestige High Dome, a WMF Perfect Plus and a Tefal Secure 5 to test the recipes.

Chapter 1

Cooking under Pressure

Unlike other types of cooking, pressure cooking uses a different process, therefore you need to make sure you understand how it works in order to be able to use the technique safely and appropriately.

How Pressure Cooking Works

At normal atmospheric pressure, water boils at 100°C, a temperature which doesn't change however long you boil the water. When cooking in a pressure cooker, the weight on the top increases the pressure inside, which raises the temperature at which the liquid boils and so speeds up the cooking. The steam created is forced through the food, tenderising it as it cooks.

It is important to remember that the cooking time depends on the size of the pieces of food, not the quantity – so 450g carrots will cook in the same time as 1kg.

What to Do

These are the basic cooking procedures but you should consult your manufacturer's leaflet for guidance on your specific cooker.

- Read through the recipe first so you know what you are doing.
- Do any pre-cooking in the open cooker.
- Put on the lid, seal it according to the model of cooker (that may mean putting on a weight or moving a switch) and bring the cooker up to pressure. Normally this can be done over a high heat, but for pasta, rice, pulses or milk dishes, it should be done over a medium heat to avoid the liquid foaming up and blocking the vent.
- Once the cooker has reached the desired pressure, reduce the heat as low as possible while still maintaining the pressure and cook for the designated time.
- Reduce the pressure (quickly by placing under cold running water, or slowly by removing from the heat source and leaving it to reduce at room temperature), as indicated in the recipe or cooking chart.

Using your Cooker Safely

When you are cooking in a pressure cooker, it is therefore important to understand a few safety issues.

- Always have at least 250–300ml liquid in the cooker when cooking under pressure.
- Do not over-fill the cooker. It should be no more than a maximum of two-thirds capacity for most dishes, but half full for soups, stews, milk products, pasta and rice, and one-third full for cereals and pulses.
- Never force the lid open when the cooker is pressurised. The pressure must be dropped; reduced either quickly or slowly, as described below, until the seal releases easily.
- Take care when moving the cooker when it is under pressure as if you knock it, the valve will open and steam will escape rapidly, which could easily scald.
- Keep the seals and valves clean at all times and replace the gasket (the rubber seal round the lid) when you find that the pressure no longer builds quickly.
- When the cooker is under pressure, never remove the weights or press down the pressure indicator (whichever your pressure cooker has) to force the pressure to reduce.
- Never use the cooker under pressure to deep-fry or shallow-fry food. Oil or melted fat under pressure would be dangerous (although it's fine to brown foods in a little fat in the open cooker).
- Never leave leftover food in the cooker. Always tip it into a suitable storage container, cool it quickly and store it the fridge or freezer.

Reducing the Pressure

- To reduce the pressure quickly, remove the pressurised cooker from the heat, place it in the sink and allow cold water to run over the lid but don't let it run over the safety valve. When the pressure is released, a slight hissing sound will be heard and the valve will drop down. On cookers with a rising line pressure guide, the guide will drop down flat with the cooker.
- To reduce the pressure slowly, simply turn off the heat (if gas) or remove the pan from the heat (if electric) and leave the cooker until the pressure subsides, which may take several minutes.

Using the Right Pots

It may seem obvious, but for those who are new to pressure cooking it is worth a reminder that you should only use appropriate bowls, tins or other utensils inside the pressure cooker, for puddings or pâtés, for example. Anything that will go into the oven or in a saucepan of boiling water is fine, so cake tins, Pyrex dishes, and so on. Do not use anything delicate or plastic.

Cleaning the Cooker

- Wash the pressure cooker in hot, soapy water, then rinse and dry thoroughly.
- If necessary, use a plastic scourer to remove any food that has stuck to the surface. Never scrub the surface with a metal scourer or you will scratch the interior and exterior.
- Some staining on the inside is normal. To remove heavy stains, boil 1 tbsp cream of tartar and water in the cooker for 20 minutes, then clean again.
- If food unfortunately boils up inside the lid, remove the gasket and wash and dry it separately, then replace it. However, you should not do this more than necessary as it shortens its life. Use a fine brush to clean the valve.

Chapter 2

How to Cook in Your Pressure Cooker

This chapter focuses on the general principles of cooking different types of meals in the pressure cooker and what you need to know when converting your own recipes. All the notes are in simple bullet points so you do not have to wade through stacks of text to find out what you need.

You will find recommended cooking times in Chapter 3 (see pages 23–25).

Soups and Stock

Apply these general principles to cooking stock or soups in your pressure cooker.
- Do not fill cooker more than half full.
- Do not use starchy vegetables, thickeners or milk products in stock.
- Cook at High pressure.
- Remove from the heat and reduce the pressure quickly under cold water.

White Stock
- To make a pale or white stock, use fresh or cooked meat bones. Break up or chop the bones, if they are large. Place them in the pressure cooker with some onions, root vegetables, celery leaves, herbs or other flavourings. Just cover with cold water, making sure the cooker is no more than half full.
- Bring to the boil in the open cooker. Skim off any scum that rises to the surface.
- Put on the lid, bring up to pressure and cook for 30 minutes for cooked bones, or 45 minutes for raw bones.
- Remove from the heat and reduce the pressure quickly under cold water.
- Strain the stock and leave to cool. Skim off any fat on the surface.

Brown Stock
- Put some onions and chopped root vegetables with a little butter or oil in the pressure cooker and fry until really well browned, stirring all the time.
- Add the chopped bones and fry them until browned again.
- Then continue to cook as for white stock (above).

Stewing and Braising

When you are cooking a stew or braising meat, the cooking time is the same even if you increase or reduce the quantities.

Cooking at High Pressure

• Put the onions and meats in the open cooker with a little oil or butter and fry until browned.
• Add the remaining ingredients and the hot liquid.
• There is little evaporation when pressure cooking so, generally, the ingredients should be less than half-covered with liquid.
• Put on the lid, bring to pressure and cook for the recommended cooking time.
• Remove from the heat and reduce the pressure quickly under cold water.
• If you need to thicken the dish, add cream or beaten eggs, do so at the end of cooking, in the open pan, and do not re-pressurise.

Poaching

• Put the ingredients in the pressure cooker with the minimum amount of cooking liquid (250–300ml). The liquid can be water, stock, wine, cider or milk (depending on the recipe).
• If you are poaching whole pieces of food (like fish), always lay them on greased foil with enough at the edges to allow for easy lifting out of the cooker. Alternatively, lay them on baking parchment in the steaming basket in the base of the cooker.
• Heat gently, then cover with the lid and bring up to pressure.
• If you are using milk (to poach fish, for example), bring up to pressure on low-medium heat to prevent the milk foaming up and blocking the vent.
• Cook for the required length of time.
• For most poached dishes, remove the cooker from the heat and reduce the pressure quickly by running under cold water .
• If you are cooking with milk, remove from the heat and allow the pressure to reduce slowly at room temperature.

Boiling

Remember, the cooking time depends on the size of the pieces of food, not the quantity – so 450g carrots will cook in the same time as 1kg.
• To calculate the cooking time, weigh the joint or bird in order to calculate the cooking time for the meat. Any vegetables will cook within that time.
• If the weight is under 1kg, allow 20–25 minutes, depending on thickness.
• If the weight is over 1kg, allow 12 minutes per 450g.

- If the meat is salted, soak it for a few hours to reduce the saltiness (unless the cooking instructions in the recipe say not to).
- Put the meat in the pan with any seasonings, such as peppercorns or herbs. Just cover with water, when possible, but make sure the cooker is no more than two-thirds full.
- Cover with the lid and bring up to High pressure over a medium heat, then reduce the heat and cook until the meat is almost done.
- Remove from the heat and reduce the pressure quickly under cold water. Add the vegetables or rice, put the lid back on and bring back to pressure. Continue to cook until both meat and vegetables are ready. That way you can ensure that neither meat nor vegetables overcook.
- When ready, reduce the pressure quickly under cold water.
- If you are serving hot, serve some of the broth with the meat or use to make a sauce. If you are serving cold, leave the meat to cool in the stock, then drain.
- Use the stock for soup.

Pot Roasting

- Don't use joints or birds bigger than 1.5kg in weight. They must fit easily into the cooker. The cooker should not be more than two-thirds full. Weigh the joint and use the cooking times in the charts on page 24.
- Always season the meat with salt and pepper, then brown it all over in a little hot oil or butter in the open cooker. Remove it from the cooker and keep to one side. Add the diced vegetables to the pan and brown them too, if you like, then take them out of the cooker and drain off the fat.
- Add 450ml stock to the pan, return the prepared vegetables, then put the meat on top. Bring up to pressure and cook for the recommended time.
- Remove from the heat and reduce the pressure quickly under cold water.
- Remove the meat and vegetables from the cooker and keep them warm for about 10–15 minutes, so the meat can rest for easier carving.
- While it is resting, season the cooking stock in the open pan. Bring it to a simmer and stir in 1 tbsp cornflour mixed with a little cold water, stirring until the stock thickens to make a gravy.

Rice, Grains and Pasta

Don't use the trivet or basket as the rice, grains and pasta need to be cooked in plenty of water to make sure they swell properly. They also need to be completely surrounded by the liquid while they are cooking so that they can absorb the liquid effectively. This is true of any food cooked in a measured amount of liquid in the pressure cooker and is known as the absorption method.

- Fill the open cooker to about one-third full with lightly salted water or stock and bring to the boil, then add the chosen grains. The cooker should be no more than half full when you've added the grains. Stir well, bring back to the boil, reduce the heat to medium, close the cooker and bring up to pressure at this reduced heat, then cook for the recommended time.
- Remove from the heat and allow the pressure to reduce slowly at room temperature.

Pulses

Pulses are also cooked in a similar way. Cooking at high pressure kills any toxins in pulses, so there is no need to boil them in the open cooker first. However, all but lentils need soaking before cooking.

- Soak any pulses except lentils in boiling water for 1 hour or in cold water for several hours, preferably overnight, before cooking.
- Drain off the soaking water and rinse the pulses. Add to the cooker with plenty of fresh cold water, making sure the cooker is no more than one-third full in total. Do not salt the water before cooking. Bring to the boil and skim any scum that rises to the surface. Reduce the heat to medium, cover with the lid and bring up to High pressure at this reduced heat. Cook for the recommended time.
- Allow the pressure to reduce slowly at room temperature.

Steaming

There are two ways to use the pressure cooker as a steamer.

You can use it as a regular steamer, in which case you put the trivet in the pressure cooker and fill with boiling water to come just below the trivet. Place the food in the basket and sit it on the trivet.

Alternatively, you can use the pressure cooker as a *bain marie*. Simply place your food in a suitable container, such as a soufflé dish or pudding basin that will fit in the pressure cooker. Stand it in the steaming basket (for easier removal) or directly in the base of the cooker containing enough boiling water to come no more than half way up the sides of the container.

Steaming Vegetables and Fish

For vegetables, particularly green ones, timing is crucial. If you pressure-cook even a minute too long, they will be discoloured and soft (that is why I quite often use the microwave to cook green vegetables and the pressure cooker for roots and tubers).

- Always cut foods to even-sized pieces so they cook evenly.
- Place the water in the base of the pan, then put the prepared vegetables in an even layer in the basket on the trivet (wire rack). Cover, bring up to pressure and cook for the

recommended time.
- For fish and vegetables, reduce the pressure quickly under cold water.

Steaming Puddings
Always cover steamed puddings securely with greaseproof paper and foil or a pudding cloth to prevent moisture getting in. For steamed puddings, you need to steam for a short while before you bring up to pressure, so you need more water than usual to allow for the extra evaporation during this period.
- Use a minimum of 900ml boiling water and add a squeeze of lemon juice to prevent discolouration of the pan. Set up the pudding, as above, and bring the water to the boil.
- Cover the pan and pre-steam, but not under pressure, for 10–15 minutes or according to the recipe to allow the food to rise and become light and airy. If you cook immediately under pressure, the result will be heavy and solid. For puddings that take over an hour to cook (like Christmas pudding), you need to make sure there is plenty of water – at least half way up the sides of the basin.
- Bring the pudding up to pressure, reduce the heat and cook for the recommended time.
- For puddings and custards, allow the pressure to reduce slowly at room temperature.

Dumplings
Never steam dumplings under pressure, or even in a completely sealed cooker, as they could rise up and block the vents. Always pressure cook your stew, then add the dumplings at the end of cooking. Steam in the closed but not sealed pan for 10–15 minutes.

Preserves
You can make delicious marmalades, jams, curds and chutneys in the pressure cooker. (In the past, I have also bottled fruit using it, too, but the latest manuals don't give instructions so I am not including this method in the book.)
- Particularly for jams, you'll get the best results if you use fruit and vegetables in perfect condition. This is not so vital for chutneys.
- Always wash and dry fruit before use and scrub the skin of citrus fruits for marmalade to remove any wax. Prepare the fruit just before use.
- Don't fill the cooker more than half full.
- For jam and marmalade, always put any pips (and fruit membranes for marmalade) in a muslin bag (or a new disposable cloth tied into a bag). Put it in with the jam or marmalade when cooking the fruit, as they contain pectin which will help the preserve to set.

- Bring the fruit or vegetables up to pressure and cook for the recommended time so they are completely soft. Do not add the sugar until the fruit or vegetables are cooked as they will not tenderise once the sugar has been added.
- Release the pressure slowly at room temperature.
- Add the sugar and cook in the open cooker until it reaches setting point for jam, or the correct consistency for chutney.

To Test for a Set
- When you think the preserve is ready and you want to test for a set, always remove the preserve from the heat. If you allow it to go on boiling, you could over cook it.
- For jams, jellies and marmalades, the easiest way is to lift up a wooden spoonful of the preserve, turn it above the preserve twice so the preserve drops off it, then hold the spoon and watch the last drop. If it stays as a jelly-like blob hanging off the spoon, setting point is reached.
- Alternatively, put a small spoonful on a cold saucer. Leave to stand for a minute then run a finger through it. If the preserve wrinkles and leaves a clear line, setting point has been reached.
- For chutneys, the mixture should be thick enough to softly plop off the spoon in a dollop, and not be runny or too stiff.

Bottling
- Once it has reached setting point, if the jam or marmalade has pieces of fruit in, leave it to cool for several minutes until a fine skin forms on the top before spooning it into jars or the fruit will all float to the top of the jars.
- Always pot your preserves in clean, dry, warm jars. To prepare them, wash them thoroughly, rinse in hot water, then then dry in a warm oven for 15 minutes. As long as they are not metal clip jars or bottles, you can also dry them in the microwave with 4 tbsp water in each jar for 2 minutes, then drain and dry upside down on sheets of kitchen paper.

Chapter 3

Cooking Times for Fresh Foods

These tables are meant as a guide only but should help you judge the correct timings for your pressure cooking. Pressure cookers and ingredients vary, so cooking cannot be an exact science. It is better to err on the side of caution and undercook. Test the food and then if it is not quite ready, you can always bring back to pressure and cook a minute or so more – you can't undo the cooking time once you've overdone it!

Ingredient	Type or preparation	Cooking time at High pressure Reduce the heat quickly unless specified
Dried pulses and cereals		
Beans	Most types	10 minutes
Butter beans		15 minutes
Chickpeas		20 minutes
Lentils	Brown, green and puy	3 minutes
	Red	Just bring to pressure
Marrowfat peas		20 minutes
Pasta shapes (large)		5 minutes
Spaghetti		3 minutes
Pearl barley		20 minutes (reduce the pressure slowly)
Rice	Brown	5 minutes
	Risotto (in measured liquid)	5 minutes (reduce the pressure slowly)
	White long-grain	3 minutes
	Wild	5 minutes
Soya beans		25 minutes
Split peas		5 minutes
Fish		
Fish	Fillets	3–4 (depending on thickness)
	Stew, casserole or curry	2 minutes
	Whole	4–7 minutes (depending on size)
Shellfish		Just bring to pressure

Fruit		
Fruit	Dried, soaked	5 minutes (reduce the pressure slowly)
	Fresh in syrup	3–5 minutes (depending on hardness) (reduce the pressure slowly)
Meat and poultry		
Bacon or gammon	Joint	8 minutes per 450g
Beef	Brisket or silverside	20 minutes per 450g
	Diced	15–20 minutes
	Tongue	15 minutes per 450g
	Topside	15 minutes per 450g
Chicken	Whole	8 minutes per 450g
	Breast, diced	5 minutes
	Portions and breasts	10 minutes
Duck	Portions	12–15 minutes
	Small whole	10 minutes per 450g
Game birds	Diced	6 minutes
	Portions	8 minutes
	Whole	8 minutes per 450g
Lamb	Diced	15 minutes
	Joint	15 minutes per 450g
Pork	Joint	15 minutes per 450g
Rabbit	Portions	15 minutes
Turkey	Diced	10 minutes
	Steaks	10 minutes
Veal	Diced	10 minutes
	Joint	12 minutes per 450g
Venison	Diced	20 minutes
	Stew, casserole or curry	15–20 minutes
Vegetables		
Artichokes, globe	Whole	6–10 minutes (depending on size)
Artichokes, Jerusalem	Whole	4 minutes
Asparagus (bundle)		2–3 minutes (depending on size)
Aubergine	Diced or baby, halved	4 minutes
Beans	Broad	2–3 minutes (depending on size)
	French, whole or cut into pieces	2 minutes
	Runner, sliced	2 minutes
Beetroot	Unpeeled	2–4 minutes (depending on size)
Broccoli		2 minutes

Brussels sprouts		2 minutes
Cabbage	Green, shredded	2 minutes
	Red or white, shredded	3 minutes
Carrots	Whole baby, sliced, diced or fingers	3 minutes
Cauliflower	Florets	2 minutes
Celery	Hearts	3 minutes
	Pieces	2 minutes
Courgettes	Baby	2 minutes
	Sliced, diced or fingers	2 minutes
Fennel	Halved or quartered	4 minutes
Kale	Shredded	3 minutes
Kohlrabi	Cut into chunks	4 minutes
Leeks	Whole baby	2 minutes
	Large, thickly sliced	3 minutes
Mangetout	Whole	1 minute
Okra	Whole	3 minutes
Onions	Whole baby or sliced	3 minutes
Parsnips	Sliced or fingers	4 minutes
Peas	Shelled	2 minutes
	Sugarsnap	2 minutes
Peppers	Sliced or chunks	3 minutes
Potatoes	New baby, whole	4–6 minutes (depending on size)
	Old, cut into chunks	4 minutes
	Large whole, scrubbed, pricked and wrapped in foil	8–10 minutes
Spinach		Use only 2 tbsp water and bring up just to High pressure and release immediately
Spring greens	Shredded	3 minutes
Sweet potatoes	Cut into chunks	5 minutes
Swede	Cut into chunks	6 minutes
Sweetcorn	On the cob	6–10 minutes (depending on size)
	Baby cobs	2 minutes
	Kernels	2 minutes
Turnips	Whole baby, or large cut into chunks	4 minutes
Yams	Cut into chunks	6 minutes
Winter squash (pumpkin, butternut, etc.)	Cut into chunks	3 minutes

Chapter 4

Storecupboard Standbys

Keeping the cupboards full means you can create meals whenever you feel like it and, as the pressure cooker is so quick, you can make meals in minutes! Here I've listed nearly everything I've used in the recipes in this book (except for fresh produce). Obviously you're not going to rush out and buy everything at once, but if you gradually build up your storecupboard, you'll always have the basis of a quick and nutritious meal. Many dry goods – like rice, pasta and flour – will keep almost indefinitely in a cool, dark, dry cupboard.

• Dried herbs and spices lose their colour and flavour when stored, so buy them in small quantities that will be used within a few months. Keep them in a cool, dark place.
• Store opened jars and bottles of pureés and sauces in the fridge to keep them fresh as long as possible.
• Never store open tins in the fridge, decant into sealable plastic containers.
• Keep fresh vegetables in the chiller box in the fridge (except roots and tubers, which are best in a rack in cool, dark cupboard).
• Always store raw meat, well wrapped, on a plate on the bottom shelf of the fridge (so no drips can fall on anything else).
• Never mix raw and cooked meat on the same shelf.
• Always cool leftovers quickly, then wrap them and store them in the fridge. Never leave food, particularly rice, at room temperature for longer than necessary.

Bottles, Jars and Tubes
Anchovy paste
Capers (pickled)
Chilli sauce (sweet)
Hoisin sauce
Honey (clear)
Lemon juice
Lime juice
Mirin or dry sherry

Oils: olive, sunflower, sesame
Olives: stoned black and green, whole and/or sliced
Passata
Syrup: golden, maple, black treacle
Soy sauce
Tomato purée
Vinegar: white or red wine, white balsamic condiment
Worcestershire sauce

Cans
Anchovies
Beans: baked, borlotti, butter, haricot, red kidney
Chickpeas
Coconut milk
Lentils
Sweetcorn
Tomatoes (chopped)

Dry Goods
Bulgur
Cornflakes
Couscous
Flour: plain, self-raising, strong white, wholemeal
Mushrooms (dried shiitake)
Naan breads
Noodles: ready-to-wok, Chinese egg, ramen, udon
Pasta: farfalle, lasagne, macaroni, papardelle, penne
Pearl barley
Popadoms (dried)
Pulses: borlotti beans, butter beans, haricot beans, pinto beans; green, red and puy
    lentils; black eye peas, chickpeas
Sugar: caster, demerara, granulated, preserving, soft light brown, soft dark brown
Tortillas (flour)

Dried Herbs, Spices, Nuts and Seeds
Basil (and a fresh pot)
Bay leaves (or fresh if you have them in your garden)
Cardamom pods

Cayenne Chilli powder
Chinese five-spice powder
Cinnamon: ground and sticks
Cloves (ground)
Coconut (desiccated)
Coriander: seeds and ground
Cumin: seeds and ground
Garam masala
Garlic cloves (or purée)
Ginger (fresh root or in a jar)
Herbs (dried mixed)
Lemongrass purée
Madras curry powder or paste
Mint
Mustard: powder and black mustard seeds
Nutmeg (preferably whole to grate but otherwise ground)
Oregano
Nuts: hazelnuts, peanuts, pecans, pine, walnuts
Paprika: smoked and sweet
Seeds: black mustard, pumpkin, sesame
Turmeric (ground)

Fridge
Bread (keeps better in the fridge)
Butter: salted and unsalted
Cheese: Cheddar, feta, halloumi, paneer, soft blue like Dolcelatte, Parmesan
Cream: single and double (or low-fat alternative)
Crème fraîche (half-fat is good)
Eggs
Milk (semi-skimmed)
Soured cream
Yoghurt (plain)

Frozen Foods
Chicken breasts
Coriander (chopped, or use fresh)
Beef or lamb mince
Onion (chopped)

Parsley (chopped, or use fresh)
Peas
Pastry: puff, filo
Shallot (chopped)
Spinach
Vegetables (mixed root)

Everyday Fresh Vegetables
Aubergine
Butternut squash
Cabbage
Carrots
Chillies
Courgettes
Cucumber
Lettuce
Mushrooms: button, chestnut, cup, portabello, oyster, shiitake
Onions: red, brown and spring
Peppers
Potatoes
Tomatoes

Chapter 5

Notes and Conversions

Those who prefer Imperial measures can use these conversions (they are approximate for ease of use).

For convenience, I sometimes use cup measures as it's so easy for things like rice or couscous. You can use American cup measuring sets, just an ordinary cup or a measuring jug. A cup is 250ml, or whatever volume fits into the space (so a cup of sugar is 225g whereas a cup of flour is 100g).

OVEN TEMPERATURES										
110°C	120°C	140°C	150°C	160°C	180°C	190°C	200°C	220°C	230°C	240°C
225°F	250°F	275°F	300°F	325°F	350°F	375°F	400°F	425°F	450°F	475°F
Gas ¼	Gas ½	Gas 1	Gas 2	Gas 3	Gas 4	Gas 5	Gas 6	Gas 7	Gas 8	Gas 9

WEIGHT										
25g	50g	75g	100g	150g	175g	200g	225g	250g	300g	450g
1oz	2oz	3oz	4oz	5oz	6oz	7oz	8oz	9oz	10oz	1lb

MEASUREMENTS										
5cm	10cm	13cm	15cm	18cm	20cm	25cm	30cm	35cm	40cm	45cm
2 in	4 in	5 in	6 in	7 in	8 in	10 in	12 in	14 in	16 in	18 in

LIQUID MEASURE										
5ml	15ml	50ml	75ml	120ml	150ml	175ml	200ml	300ml	450ml	600ml
1 tsp	1 tbsp	2 fl oz	3 fl oz	4 fl oz	5 fl oz	6 fl oz	7 fl oz	½pt	¾pt	1pt

Notes on the recipes

The ingredients are listed in the order in which they are used in the recipe.
All spoon measures are level unless otherwise stated. 1 tbsp = 15ml; 1 tsp = 5ml.
Eggs and vegetables are medium unless otherwise stated.

Always wash, peel, core and deseed, if necessary, fresh produce before use and cut into even-sized pieces. But deseeding fresh chillies is up to you (some say it reduces the heat to remove the seeds and white pith. If you like heat, leave them in).

Seasoning is very much a matter of personal taste. Taste the food as you cook and adjust to suit your own palate.

Fresh herbs are great for adding flavour and colour. Pots of basil and parsley for your windowsill are particularly good (they keep best if left in the plastic wrapper). The others are best bought in bunches and kept in the chiller box in the fridge.

For quickness, use garlic and ginger purée instead of crushing or grating your own.

All can and packet sizes are approximate as they vary from brand to brand.

Cooking times are approximate and should be used as a guide only. Always check food is piping hot and cooked through before serving.

When the oven or grill is necessary to finish a dish, always preheat it and cook on the shelf just above the centre of the oven (this isn't necessary in a fan oven which heats very quickly and the heat is similar throughout the oven) or 5cm from the heat source for the grill, unless otherwise stated.

Remember that in pressure cooking, it is the size of the pieces of food that determines its cooking time, not the quantity. One portion will take as long as four.

Always make sure you have at least 250–300ml liquid in the cooker (even if you are only cooking a small quantity) or the food might stick. However, liquid does not evaporate much when cooking under pressure so for soups, stews and casseroles you don't need as much as when cooking conventionally.

Chapter 6

Soups

Soups can be elegant and sophisticated or a great way to use up the odds and ends in your fridge. Ones that would take ages to simmer conventionally can be cooked in minutes, literally, in the pressure cooker.

For the quickest vegetable soup, simply dig out all the bits and pieces sitting in the chiller box, left over from when you had one too many of the vegetable you were cooking. Peel and chop or shred as appropriate and put in the pressure cooker. Cover with vegetable stock (no more than half to two-thirds full). Add a sprinkling of dried herbs and some salt and pepper. Put on the lid, bring up to High pressure, then reduce the heat and cook for 10 minutes (to ensure even large pieces of vegetable are really tender). Remove from the heat and reduce the pressure quickly under cold water. Purée in a blender or food processor. Return to the pan, taste, re-season and serve – simple!

This is the soup to make when you have a glut of home-grown tomatoes. You could just make 4 crostini and stand one up in each bowl, resting on the edge, to garnish, but I prefer to make a plateful to serve alongside for a light meal.

Serves 4 | Preparation time: 20 minutes | Cooking time: 5 minutes | Vegetarian

Fresh Tomato and Basil Soup with Pizza Crostini

1 ciabatta loaf

Olive oil, for brushing

750g ripe tomatoes, skinned and chopped

1 banana shallot, chopped

1 tsp caster sugar

4–5 tbsp tomato purée

1 tbsp white balsamic condiment

300ml vegetable stock

4 tbsp chopped fresh basil

Salt and freshly ground black pepper

½ tsp dried oregano

100g mozzarella cheese, grated

To garnish

4 tiny sprigs of basil

1. Preheat the grill.

2. Cut a 1cm thick slice from each end of the ciabatta loaf and make them into breadcrumbs to use for another recipe. Cut the remaining ciabatta bread into 12 slices. Brush with olive oil and grill on both sides until golden. Set aside.

3. Put the tomatoes, shallot, sugar, 2 tbsp of the tomato purée, the white balsamic condiment and stock in the pressure cooker.

4. Cover with the lid and bring up to High pressure, then reduce the heat and cook for 5 minutes.

5. Remove from the heat and reduce the pressure quickly under cold water.

6. Purée in a blender or food processor with 2 tbsp of the chopped basil. Rinse out the pan. Return the soup to the pan, taste and season with salt and pepper. Reheat gently without allowing the soup to boil.

7. Meanwhile, put the toasted ciabatta back on the grill rack. Spread each slice with a little of the remaining tomato purée, sprinkle with the oregano, then top with the mozzarella. Grill for a few minutes, just until the cheese melts and bubbles. Sprinkle with the remaining chopped basil, gently pressing so it adheres to the cheese.

8. Ladle the soup into warm bowls and garnish each one with a tiny sprig of fresh basil. Serve with the pizza crostini.

This is a good way to use up the tougher outer leaves of a lettuce. The soup has a slightly peppery taste that goes really well with eggs. Serve with warm multi-grain bread rolls for a substantial starter or a light lunch or supper.

Serves 4 | Preparation time: 10 minutes | Cooking time: 10 minutes | Vegetarian

Lettuce, Watercress and Spring Onion Soup with Poached Eggs

1 bunch of watercress (about 75g)

A knob of butter

1 bunch of spring onions, trimmed and roughly chopped

1 large potato, peeled and diced

8 outer leaves of a soft round lettuce, roughly shredded

750ml vegetable stock

1 tbsp chopped fresh parsley, plus extra for garnish

1 tbsp chopped fresh thyme

Salt and freshly ground black pepper

90ml double cream

4 eggs

1 tbsp lemon juice

1. Reserve 4 tiny sprigs of watercress for garnish and roughly chop the remainder.

2. Melt the butter in the pressure cooker and fry the spring onions for 2 minutes, stirring, until softened but not browned. Add the potato, lettuce, stock, parsley and thyme. Season with salt and pepper.

3. Cover with the lid and bring up to High pressure, then reduce the heat and cook for 5 minutes.

4. Remove from the heat and reduce the pressure quickly under cold water.

5. Purée in a blender or food processor with 60ml of the cream. Rinse out the pan. Return the soup to the pan, and reheat but do not boil.

6. Poach the eggs in gently simmering water with the lemon juice added, or in an egg poacher, until cooked to your liking.

7. As soon as the eggs are just about ready, ladle the soup into warm open soup plates and gently lay a poached egg in each plate. Add a swirl of cream around the eggs and serve.

For quickness, you can use a can of cooked haricot beans. Simply start at step 5 of the recipe. You can use any aniseed-flavoured liqueur – even ouzo! Serve the soup with warm ciabatta bread with olives.

Serves 4–6 | Preparation time: 10 minutes, plus soaking | Cooking time: 27 minutes | Vegetarian

Haricot Bean and Fennel Soup with Pernod and Crispy Sage

100g dried haricot beans, soaked in cold water for several hours or overnight

1 tbsp olive oil

1 large onion, finely chopped

1 garlic clove, crushed

1 head of fennel, finely chopped, green fronds reserved

400g can of chopped tomatoes

750g vegetable stock

3 tbsp Pernod

1 tbsp tomato purée

1 tsp clear honey

1 tbsp chopped fresh sage

Salt and freshly ground black pepper

To garnish

Sunflower oil, for frying

12 fresh sage leaves

1. Drain the beans and place in the pressure cooker. Cover with fresh water so that the cooker is no more than one-third full. Bring to the boil in the open cooker, and skim off any scum that comes to the surface, if necessary. Reduce the heat to medium.

2. Cover with the lid and bring up to High pressure at this reduced heat, then cook for 20 minutes.

3. Remove from the heat and allow the pressure to reduce slowly at room temperature.

4. Drain the beans. Rinse and dry the pressure cooker.

5. Heat the oil in the pressure cooker and fry the onion, garlic and fennel gently for 2 minutes, stirring, until softened but not browned. Add the remaining ingredients, seasoning with salt and pepper.

6. Cover with the lid and bring up to High pressure, then reduce the heat and cook for 5 minutes.

7. Remove from the heat and reduce the pressure quickly under cold water. Taste and re-season.

8. Meanwhile, heat a little oil for shallow-frying in a frying pan until very hot but not smoking. Add the sage and fry for a few seconds just until the leaves are bright green and they've stopped sizzling. Remove immediately with a slotted spoon and drain on kitchen paper.

9. Ladle the soup into warm bowls and garnish with the sage.

Pistou is a French version of pesto. Here I've made it with coriander rather than the more usual basil as the flavour complements the spices in the soup so perfectly.

Serves 6 | Preparation time: 25 minutes | Cooking time: 10 minutes | Vegetarian

Spiced Carrot and Sweet Potato Soup with Coriander Pistou

For the soup

A knob of butter

1 large onion, chopped

3 large carrots, peeled and chopped

500g sweet potatoes, peeled and diced

$\frac{1}{2}$ tsp ground cumin

$\frac{1}{2}$ tsp sweet paprika

1 tsp harissa paste

$\frac{1}{2}$ tsp dried mixed herbs

1 litre vegetable stock

Salt and freshly ground black pepper

For the pistou

A large handful of coriander leaves

50g pine nuts

2 garlic cloves, crushed

Finely grated zest of 1 lime

1 tsp lime juice

5 tbsp olive oil

1. Heat the butter in the pressure cooker and fry the onion and carrots, stirring, for 2 minutes until lightly golden. Stir in the sweet potatoes and the remaining soup ingredients, seasoning with salt and pepper.

2. Cover with the lid and bring up to High pressure, then reduce the heat and cook for 8 minutes.

3. Remove from the heat and reduce the pressure quickly under cold water.

4. Purée the soup in a blender or food processor. Rinse out the pan. Return the soup to the pan, taste and re-season, if necessary.

5. Meanwhile, make the pistou. Put all the ingredients in a blender or food processor and run the machine until the mixture forms a paste, stopping and scraping down the sides as necessary. Season to taste with salt and pepper.

6. Ladle the soup into warm bowls and serve topped with a spoonful of the pistou.

I like the flavour of mixed roots in this soup, but you can use just one whole bunch of raw beetroot if you prefer. It's also delicious served chilled.

Serves 6 | Preparation time: 15 minutes | Cooking time: 10 minutes | Vegetarian

Beetroot and Carrot Borscht with Soured Cream and Dill

3 large carrots, peeled and coarsely grated

3 large beetroot, peeled and coarsely grated

1 red onion, coarsely grated

1 celery stick, strings removed and coarsely grated

900ml vegetable stock

3 tbsp red wine vinegar

1 tsp soft light brown sugar

1 bay leaf

½ tsp ground cinnamon

Salt and freshly ground black pepper

For the soured cream

4–6 tbsp soured cream or crème fraîche

2 tbsp chopped fresh dill

1 tsp caraway seeds

1. Put the grated vegetables in the pressure cooker. Stir in the stock, vinegar, sugar, bay leaf, cinnamon, a little salt and a good grinding of black pepper.

2. Cover with the lid and bring up to High pressure, then reduce the heat and cook for 8 minutes.

3. Meanwhile, mix together the soured cream and dill, season lightly with salt and pepper and chill until ready to serve.

4. Remove the pressure cooker from the heat and reduce the pressure quickly under cold water.

5. Discard the bay leaf. Taste and re-season the soup, if necessary. Ladle into warm bowls and serve topped with a spoonful of the dill soured cream and a sprinkling of caraway seeds.

Minestrone is everyone's favourite vegetable soup! You can omit either the haricot beans or the pasta for a slightly less filling dish but it's really good served as it is, followed by some Italian prosciutto, or cheese and a crisp salad. For true vegetarians, use a vegetarian Parmesan-style cheese.

Serves 4–6 | Preparation time: 10 minutes | Cooking time: 10 minutes | Vegetarian

Minestrone Soup

1 tbsp olive oil

1 onion, chopped

1 carrot, peeled and finely chopped

1 small turnip, peeled and finely chopped

1/4 small green cabbage, finely shredded, discarding any thick stump

50g fine green beans, cut into short lengths

1 tbsp tomato purée

400g can of chopped tomatoes

1 litre vegetable stock

1 bay leaf

4 semi-dried tomatoes from a jar, chopped

1 tbsp semi-dried tomato oil from the jar

1 small handful of short-cut macaroni

Salt and freshly ground black pepper

2 tbsp chopped fresh basil

To serve

Freshly grated Parmesan cheese

1. Heat the oil in the pressure cooker, add the onion and fry for 2 minutes, stirring, until soft but not browned. Add all the remaining ingredients except the basil, seasoning with salt and pepper.

2. Cover with the lid and bring up to High pressure, then reduce the heat and cook for 8 minutes.

3. Remove from the heat and reduce the pressure quickly under cold water.

4. Discard the bay leaf. Add the basil, taste and re-season, if necessary. Ladle into soup bowls and serve sprinkled liberally with grated Parmesan cheese.

This hearty soup is packed with flavour. For a more substantial
meal, serve two croûtes per person and add a slice of ham to
them before topping with the cheese, if you like.

Serves 4 | Preparation time: 10 minutes | Cooking time: 14–19 minutes | Vegetarian

French Onion Soup

25g butter

450g onions, halved and sliced

2 tsp caster sugar

2 tbsp port (optional)

1 litre vegetable stock

1 bouquet garni

Salt and freshly ground black
  pepper

4 diagonal slices of baguette

4 small handfuls grated Cheddar
  cheese

1. Melt the butter in the pressure cooker. Fry the onions
   gently for 5–10 minutes, stirring frequently, until softened
   and lightly golden. Stir in the sugar and fry for about 5
   minutes, stirring, until the onions are richly browned and
   caramelised.

2. Add the port, if using, the stock and bouquet garni and
   season with salt and pepper.

3. Cover with the lid and bring up to High pressure, then
   reduce the heat and cook for 4 minutes.

4. Remove from the heat and allow the pressure to reduce
   slowly at room temperature.

5. Discard the bouquet garni. Taste and re-season, if
   necessary.

6. Meanwhile, preheat the grill and toast the bread on both
   sides. Top with the cheese and grill until melted.

7. Ladle the soup into bowls and float a slice of toasted cheese
   in each bowl.

This is equally delicious made with a large head of broccoli instead of the cauliflower, but peel the broccoli stalk, then chop it and add to the pot too – don't waste anything!

Serves 4 | Preparation time: 8 minutes | Cooking time: 7 minutes | Vegetarian

Cauliflower and Blue Cheese Soup

A knob of butter

1 onion, chopped

1 small cauliflower, trimmed and cut into florets, discarding the leaves

1 large potato, peeled and diced

600ml vegetable stock

1 tsp chopped fresh thyme

1 bay leaf

Salt and freshly ground black pepper

150ml milk

100g Stilton or other blue cheese, crumbled

150ml single cream

To garnish

A little chopped fresh parsley

1. Melt the butter in the pressure cooker. Fry the onion gently for 2 minutes, stirring, until softened but not browned. Add the cauliflower, potato and stock. Add the thyme and bay leaf and season with salt and pepper.

2. Cover with the lid and bring up to High pressure, then reduce the heat and cook for 5 minutes.

3. Remove from the heat and allow the pressure to reduce slowly at room temperature.

4. Discard the bay leaf. Purée the soup in a blender or food processor with the milk and cheese. Rinse out the pan, then tip the soup back into the pan. Stir in the cream and heat through but do not allow the soup to boil. Taste and re-season, if necessary. Ladle into bowls and serve garnished with a little chopped parsley.

This velvety soup is traditionally served chilled but it is equally delicious served hot on a cold winter's day. It usually calls for the white part of leek only but I like to add the green too.

Serves 4 | Preparation time: 10 minutes | Cooking time: 12 minutes | Vegetarian

Vichyssoise

A large knob of butter

2 good-sized leeks, well washed and sliced

450g potatoes, peeled and diced

1 bay leaf

750ml vegetable stock

Salt and freshly ground black pepper

2 egg yolks

150ml single cream, plus extra to garnish

To garnish

A few snipped fresh chives

1. Melt the butter in the pressure cooker. Add the leeks and fry gently, stirring, for 4 minutes until softened but don't allow them to brown. Add the potatoes, bay leaf and stock. Season with a little salt and plenty of pepper.

2. Cover with the lid and bring up to High pressure, then reduce the heat and cook for 8 minutes.

3. Remove from the heat and allow the pressure to reduce slowly at room temperature.

4. Discard the bay leaf. Purée the soup in a blender or food processor. Rinse out the pan. Then, for smoothest results (although not compulsory), rub the soup through a sieve and return it to the pan.

5. Whisk the egg yolks with the cream and strain into the soup. Heat, stirring, until it thickens slightly, but do not allow it to boil. Taste and re-season, if necessary.

6. Leave the soup to cool, then chill until ready to serve. Ladle into chilled soup cups and garnish with a swirl of cream and a few snipped chives.

The addition of some soaked dried mushrooms really enhances the flavour and makes this soup something special. You can omit them if you prefer but it won't taste so good!

Serves 4 | Preparation time: 8 minutes, plus soaking | Cooking time: 9 minutes

Chinese Chicken, Mushroom and Noodle Soup

2 tbsp dried, sliced shiitake mushrooms

120ml boiling water

1 chicken portion

1 onion, washed and quartered, but not peeled

1 thick slice of fresh root ginger

1 carrot, peeled and roughly chopped

1 bay leaf

750ml chicken stock

50g fresh shiitake or button mushrooms, sliced

1 tbsp soy sauce

1 nest of fine Chinese egg noodles, roughly broken up

2 tbsp mirin or dry sherry

To garnish

A few fresh chive stalks

1. Put the dried mushrooms in a bowl. Cover with the boiling water and leave to soak for 20 minutes.

2. Meanwhile, put the chicken in the pressure cooker with the onion, ginger, carrot, bay leaf and stock.

3. Cover with the lid and bring up to High pressure, then reduce the heat and cook for 8 minutes.

4. Remove from the heat and reduce the pressure quickly under cold water.

5. Lift the chicken out of the pan. Cut all the meat off the bones. Discard the bones and skin and chop the meat. Strain the stock and return it to the pressure cooker. Add the soaked mushrooms and their water and all the remaining ingredients except the mirin or sherry. Bring back to High pressure and cook for 1 minute.

6. Remove from the heat and reduce the pressure quickly under cold water.

7. Stir in the mirin or sherry, taste and add more soy sauce, if necessary. Ladle into bowls and serve each one garnished with two crossed chive stalks.

Chorizo sausage is so versatile, it imparts rich colour and flavour to many dishes including this peasant-style soup. You can buy it ready-diced for convenience. But for best results don't use the thinly sliced variety that's usually served cold.

Serves 4 | Preparation time: 25 minutes | Cooking time: 11 minutes

Chorizo Sausage, Cabbage and Potato Soup

1 red pepper

2 tbsp olive oil, plus extra for garnishing

1 onion, finely chopped

1 large garlic clove, crushed

75g chorizo, diced

$\frac{1}{2}$ tsp smoked paprika

A pinch of crushed dried chillies

2 large potatoes, peeled and diced

$\frac{1}{2}$ small green cabbage, chopped

1 tsp chopped fresh rosemary

750ml chicken or vegetable stock

Salt and freshly ground black pepper

To garnish

4 tiny sprigs of rosemary (with flowers when in season)

To serve

Crème fraîche (optional)

1. Roast the pepper either on a long fork over a gas flame or under a preheated grill, turning occasionally until blackened all over. Place in a plastic bag, leave to cool for 5 minutes, then peel, halve, deseed and cut into thin strips.

2. Heat the oil in the pressure cooker and gently fry the onion and garlic, stirring, for 2 minutes. Add the chorizo and cook, stirring, for a further 1 minute. Add the remaining ingredients, seasoning with salt and pepper.

3. Cover with the lid and bring up to High pressure, then reduce the heat and cook for 8 minutes.

4. Remove from the heat and reduce the pressure quickly under cold water.

5. Taste and re-season, if necessary. Ladle into warm bowls, trickle a little olive oil over each and stand a tiny sprig of rosemary in the soup at the edge of each bowl. Serve with crème fraîche to spoon in, if you like.

This is best made with fresh corn as you put the stripped cobs in the pot as well for added flavour (then take them out before you finish the soup). However, you can use a 350g can of sweetcorn for quickness. For vegetarians, omit the bacon.

Serves 4–6 | Preparation time: 15 minutes | Cooking time: 6 minutes

Bacon and Corn Chowder

3 corn cobs

50g unsmoked bacon lardons

1 large onion, finely chopped

1 large potato, peeled and diced

2 celery sticks, chopped

500ml vegetable stock

Salt and freshly ground black pepper

250ml milk

2 tbsp dried milk powder

4 tbsp double cream

To garnish

A little chopped fresh parsley

1. Remove the husks and silks from each corn cob, if necessary. Hold the cobs one at a time upright on a board and slice down on all sides to remove the kernels.

2. Dry-fry the lardons in the pressure cooker, stirring until the fat runs. Add the onion and cook, stirring, for 1 minute until softening but not browning. Add the corn kernels, the stripped cobs, potato, celery, stock and a little salt and pepper.

3. Cover with the lid and bring up to High pressure, then reduce the heat and cook for 5 minutes.

4. Remove from the heat and reduce the pressure quickly under cold water.

5. Discard the corn cobs. Blend the milk with the milk powder and stir into the cooker. Simmer for 2 minutes in the open pan. Stir in the cream, taste and re-season. Serve sprinkled with parsley.

To remove the strings from celery sticks, simply scrape the outside of the stalks with a potato peeler. It's worth doing as that means you don't have to sieve the soup after puréeing to remove the stringy bits.

Serves 4 | Preparation time: 15 minutes | Cooking time: 15 minutes

Split Pea and Crispy Bacon Soup

4 rashers of smoked streaky bacon, rind removed

2 leeks, trimmed and chopped

1 celery stick, strings removed and chopped

1 bouquet garni

A good grating of freshly grated nutmeg

100g green split peas

1 litre chicken or vegetable stock

2 tbsp chopped fresh mint

Salt and freshly ground black pepper

1. Chop 2 rashers of the bacon. Fry in the open pressure cooker for about 2 minutes, stirring until the fat runs. Add the leeks and fry, stirring, for 2 minutes to soften. Reserve half the mint for garnish, seasoning with salt and pepper, then add all the remaining ingredients to the pan. Bring to the boil, then reduce the heat to medium.

2. Cover with the lid and bring up to High pressure over a medium heat, then cook for 12 minutes.

3. Remove from the heat and allow the pressure to reduce slowly at room temperature.

4. Discard the bouquet garni. Purée in a blender or food processor. Rinse out the pan, then return the soup to the pan. Reheat gently, taste and re-season.

5. Meanwhile, dry-fry or grill the remaining bacon until crisp. Drain on kitchen paper. Chop into small pieces.

6. Ladle the soup into serving bowls. Add a small cluster of the crispy bacon and sprinkle with the reserved mint.

This is based on the traditional hearty lamb soup, Scotch Broth. The quantities aren't crucial, so you can add any vegetables you have to hand. It's hearty and nutritious and great with plenty of crusty bread for lunch or supper.

Serves 4 | Preparation time: 10 minutes | Cooking time: 50 minutes

Anything Goes Lamb and Barley Broth

1 meaty roast lamb leg or shoulder bone

1.2 litres water

A good handful of pearl barley

1 tbsp chicken stock concentrate

1 onion, chopped

2 carrots, peeled and finely diced

1 small parsnip, peeled and finely diced

1 potato, peeled and finely diced

A handful of chopped, shredded spring greens or cabbage

1 large bay leaf

Salt and freshly ground black pepper

A handful of fresh parsley, finely chopped

1. Break up the lamb bone at any joints. Place in the pressure cooker and pour in the water. Bring to the boil in the open cooker and skim any scum that rises to the surface, if necessary.

2. Cover with the lid and bring up to High, then reduce the heat and cook for 30 minutes.

3. Remove from the heat and reduce the pressure quickly under cold water.

4. Leave the bone to cool in the liquid, then remove all the meat from the bone, discarding any fat. Skim off the fat from the stock.

5. Return the meat to the stock and add all the remaining ingredients except the parsley.

6. Cover with the lid and bring up to High pressure, then reduce the heat and cook for 20 minutes.

7. Remove from the heat and allow the pressure to reduce slowly at room temperature.

8. Discard the bay leaf. Stir in the parsley, taste and re-season, if necessary. Reheat gently and serve hot.

Chapter 7

Starters and Light Bites

Your pressure cooker can make a whole selection of starters and light meals. I've tried to give you a selection here to show you just how versatile it can be, but be prepared to experiment. Where I've use game, for instance, for a potted meat recipe, you could do exactly the same recipe with stewing beef. The Bagna Cauda on page 57 is made with the artichokes but would be just as good served with the steamed asparagus on page 58. Some of these recipes can be made in advance and kept in the fridge – such as the Chicken Liver and Mushroom Pâté on page 61. Others can be quickly thrown together in an instant – see how quickly you can serve up garlic mushrooms (page 56). It is another lesson in discovering how easy it is to make your pressure cooker work for you. It isn't just for cooking a soup or stews; it can do so much more!

Pressure cooking the aubergine means it cooks in next to no time and becomes beautifully soft so that you can purée it for this pâté. It's a version of the delicious Middle-Eastern favourite baba ganoush.

Serves 4–6 | Preparation time: 10 minutes, plus chilling | Cooking time: 13–17 minutes | Vegetarian

Aubergine and Cream Cheese Pâté

1 large aubergine, halved

A sprinkling of lemon juice

2 spring onions, chopped

50g soft white cheese

1 large garlic clove, crushed

5 tbsp olive oil, plus extra for drizzling

A small handful of fresh basil leaves, chopped

A small handful of fresh flatleaf parsley, chopped

1 tsp lemon juice

Salt and freshly ground black pepper

To serve

4–6 pitta breads

1. Put the aubergine in the steaming basket on the trivet in the pressure cooker. Add 250ml water and the lemon juice to the cooker.

2. Cover with the lid and bring up to High pressure, then reduce the heat and cook for 5 minutes.

3. Remove from the heat and reduce the pressure quickly under cold water.

4. Remove the aubergine from the pressure cooker and leave it to cool. Pull off the skin.

5. Put the flesh in a blender or food processor with the chopped white part of the onions, the cheese, garlic, 5 tbsp olive oil and the herbs. Run the machine until the mixture is roughly puréed, stopping and scraping down the sides as necessary. Sharpen with a little lemon juice and season to taste with salt and pepper.

6. Spoon into a serving bowl and garnish with the chopped green part of the spring onions and a drizzle of olive oil. Chill until ready to serve.

7. Meanwhile, brush the pittas on the outside with olive oil and heat a griddle pan. Griddle the pittas on both sides until toasted and scored with brown lines. Cut into thick slices and serve with the pâté.

A popular favourite dip that is simple and very economical to make, particularly if you cook your own chickpeas.

Serves 6 | Preparation time: 10 minutes | Cooking time: 25 minutes | Vegetarian

Hummus

150g dried chickpeas, soaked for several hours or overnight, then drained

600ml boiling water

2 large garlic cloves, crushed

4 tbsp lemon juice

5 tbsp olive oil, plus extra for garnish

4 tbsp tahini (sesame seed paste)

Salt and freshly ground black pepper

To garnish

A few torn flatleaf parsley leaves

A sprinkling of cayenne

To serve

Warm pitta breads, cut into strips

Pickled chillies and black olives

1. Drain the chickpeas and place in the pressure cooker with the boiling water. Bring to the boil, then skim any froth from the surface. Reduce heat to medium.

2. Cover with the lid and bring up to High pressure over a medium heat, then cook for 20 minutes.

3. Remove from the heat and reduce the pressure quickly under cold water.

4. Drain the chickpeas, reserving the cooking water.

5. Tip the cooked chickpeas into the blender or food processor. Add the lemon juice, olive oil and tahini. Purée until smooth (or keep a bit chunky if you prefer), adding enough of the cooking water to give a thick, creamy consistency. Season with salt and pepper, then transfer to a shallow serving dish.

6. Drizzle with a little olive oil. Garnish with the parsley and a dusting of cayenne. Serve with warm pitta breads cut into strips, pickled chillies and black olives.

Camembert en boite is a very trendy starter these days but it usually means putting the oven on just to melt the cheese, which is not eco-friendly at all! I've found that it works brilliantly in the pressure cooker and only takes a few minutes! The wooden boxes are more robust than cardboard ones.

Serves 4 | Preparation time: 15 minutes | Cooking time: 5 minutes | Vegetarian

Camembert Melted in the Box with Vegetable Dippers

For the dippers

1 round camembert in a wooden box

1 large garlic clove, halved

1 tbsp dry cider or white wine

1 tbsp chopped fresh thyme

Freshly ground black pepper

To serve

2 carrots, peeled, cut into matchsticks

2 celery sticks, cut into matchsticks

2 red peppers, cut into matchsticks

1 bunch of breakfast radishes, trimmed with a small stalk left

Warm, crusty French bread

1. Unwrap the camembert and rub all over with the garlic. Put the cheese back in the box. Use a metal skewer to make holes all over the top of the cheese right down through it. Spoon over the cider or wine. Smear it with the back of a spoon to help it into the holes. Sprinkle with the thyme and plenty of pepper. Replace the lid. Wrap the box tightly in foil to seal completely (so the steam doesn't get in).

2. Put 300ml water in the cooker. Place the cheese in the steaming basket on the trivet so it is well away from the water.

3. Cover with the lid and bring up to High pressure, then reduce the heat and cook for 5 minutes.

4. Remove from the heat and reduce the pressure quickly under cold water.

5. Carefully lift out the box, unwrap and place on a serving plate. Remove the lid (the cheese should feel wobbly under the crust) and arrange the dippers around. Serve straight away with a basket of warm crusty French bread, too, to dip into the cheese.

Make the sauce and cook the potatoes for the gnocchi at the same time in this simple supper dish. Serve it with some crusty bread and a crisp green salad. The gnocchi are also good just drizzled with melted butter, flavoured with chopped rosemary and then sprinkled with the cheese.

Serves 4 | Preparation time: 15 minutes | Cooking time: 9 minutes | Vegetarian

Potato Gnocchi with Fresh Tomato and Basil Sauce

For the sauce

4 large ripe tomatoes

4 spring onions, chopped

1 large garlic clove, crushed

A pinch of dried chilli flakes (optional)

Salt and freshly ground black pepper

2 tbsp tomato purée

A large pinch of caster sugar

2 tbsp chopped fresh basil, plus a few torn leaves for garnish

For the gnocchi

900g floury potatoes, peeled and cut into walnut-sized chunks

2 eggs, beaten

225g plain flour, plus extra for dusting

¼ tsp freshly grated nutmeg

To serve

Extra virgin olive oil

Freshly grated Parmesan cheese

1. Make a cross cut into the rounded ends of the tomatoes. Place in a bowl and cover with boiling water. Leave for 30 seconds, drain and remove the skins. Roughly chop the tomato flesh and place in a 900ml heatproof basin. Add the remaining sauce ingredients except the basil. Cover the bowl with foil, twisting and folding under the rim to secure.

2. Put about 600ml water in the pressure cooker. Add the bowl to one side of the pan. Put the potato pieces around the bowl in the water and sprinkle them lightly with salt.

3. Cover with the lid and bring up to High pressure, then reduce the heat and cook for 6 minutes.

4. Remove from the heat and reduce the pressure quickly under cold water.

5. Lift out the basin of tomato sauce, beat well with a wooden spoon to a pulp and stir in the basil. Re-cover with the foil and keep warm. Drain the potatoes and return them to the pan and dry out over a low heat. Tip out into a bowl. Rinse out the pan, three-quarters fill with water, add a pinch of salt and put back on the heat to boil.

6. Mash the potatoes well, then work in the eggs, flour, a good grating of nutmeg and some seasoning to form a soft but not too sticky dough. With floured hands, shape the mixture into 48–50 walnut-sized balls. When the water is boiling, drop in the gnocchi and boil for about 3 minutes until they all rise to the surface. Remove with a slotted spoon and drain on kitchen paper.

7. Divide the gnocchi between four shallow bowls. Drizzle with a little olive oil, then spoon the tomato sauce over the top and sprinkle with grated Parmesan. Garnish with a few torn basil leaves and serve.

If you go wild mushroom picking (and only do so if you know what you are looking for), this is a wonderful way of cooking them. It is particularly good with chanterelles. All the ones suggested below are available cultivated. If necessary, use white cup with a few soaked dried shiitake or chanterelle for flavour.

Serves 4 | Preparation time: 5 minutes | Cooking time: 10 minutes | Vegetarian

Mixed Garlic Mushrooms in Cider and Cream

A large knob of butter

2 garlic cloves, crushed

350g mixed mushrooms (such as oyster, chestnut, shiitake, chanterelle, white cup etc.), trimmed and thickly sliced

250ml dry cider

Salt and freshly ground black pepper

120ml double cream

2 tbsp chopped fresh parsley

4 diagonally cut slices ciabatta

Olive oil, for brushing

1. Melt the butter in the pressure cooker and stir in the garlic. Add the mushrooms and toss gently. Pour over the cider and add a little salt and pepper.

2. Cover with a lid and bring up to Low pressure, then reduce the heat and cook for 5 minutes.

3. Remove from the heat and reduce the pressure quickly under cold water.

4. Carefully lift out the mushrooms with a slotted spoon. Boil the liquid rapidly in the open cooker for about 4 minutes until the liquid is reduced by half.

5. Stir in the cream and half the parsley and boil for a further minute. Taste and re-season, if necessary. Return the mushrooms to the sauce and heat through.

6. Meanwhile brush the ciabatta slices with olive oil on both sides and grill until golden. Place on plates and spoon the mushrooms and sauce over. Sprinkle with the parsley and serve at once.

This unctuous anchovy sauce is the perfect dip to enjoy with the artichoke leaves and the succulent bases. You can, of course, just serve them with melted butter or hollandaise sauce (see page 58) if you prefer.

Serves 4 | Preparation time: 20 minutes | Cooking time: 6–10 minutes

Globe Artichokes with Bagna Cauda

4 even-sized globe artichokes

300ml boiling water

A large pinch of salt

2 tbsp lemon juice

For the bagna cauda

2 x 50g cans of anchovy fillets, drained and chopped, reserving the oil

2 garlic cloves, crushed

100g butter, diced

1 tbsp chopped fresh rosemary

6 tbsp double cream

To serve

Crusty bread

1. Twist off the stalks from the artichokes (the strings will come away with the stalks). Trim the bases, if necessary, so they will stand upright. Trim the tips of the leaves with scissors and cut the pointed tops level.

2. Put the boiling water in the pressure cooker with the salt and lemon juice. Add the artichokes to the cooker.

3. Cover with the lid and bring up to High pressure, then reduce the heat and cook for 6 minutes.

4. Remove from the heat and reduce the pressure quickly under cold water.

5. Check that one of the outer leaves pulls away easily. If not, pressure cook the artichokes for a minute or two longer. Drain the artichokes.

6. Put the anchovies, their oil, the garlic, butter and rosemary in the pressure cooker and cook gently, stirring with a wire whisk to blend the anchovies into the oil and butter. When hot and smooth, stir in the cream. Remove from the heat.

7. If liked, pull out the small leaves in the top centre of each artichoke, then scoop out the feathery choke with a spoon (or leave your guests to do this). Stand an artichoke on each of four small plates. Spoon the warm bagna cauda into four warmed little ramekins and place alongside.

8. To eat, pull off a leaf at a time, dip in the bagna cauda, then pull the fleshy part through the teeth and discard the rest. When all the large leaves have been eaten, remove the small leaves and chokes, if not done before, then trim the fleshy base with a knife and fork and eat it cut into chunks. Mop up any remaining bagna cauda with crusty bread.

This is a good example of making the microwave work alongside the pressure cooker. You can make this in a saucepan but using the microwave is very quick indeed. Just make sure you cook in 10-second bursts after the first minute, or it will curdle. If this happens, add 1 tbsp hot water and whisk well.

Serves 4 | Preparation time: 10 minutes | Cooking time: 4½–5½ minutes | Vegetarian

Asparagus with Semi-dried Tomato Hollandaise

100g butter

1 tbsp lemon juice

2 eggs, beaten

2 tbsp tomato oil from the semi-dried tomatoes

A pinch of cayenne

4 semi-dried tomatoes in oil, drained and finely chopped

A large pinch of caster sugar

Salt and freshly ground black pepper

350g thin asparagus spears

A little sweet paprika

1. Put the butter in a microwave-safe bowl. Cover the bowl with kitchen paper (to prevent splattering). Melt the butter on Full-power for 30–50 seconds until almost melted. Stir to completely melt the butter, then whisk in the lemon juice, eggs, tomato oil and cayenne.

2. Microwave on Full-power for 1 minute. Whisk well. Continue to microwave in 10-seconds bursts (no more), whisking after each burst until thick, smooth and glossy. Don't overcook. Whisk in the chopped semi-dried tomatoes and season with sugar, cayenne, salt and pepper to taste. Sharpen with more lemon juice, if liked.

3. Trim off the last 2.5cm from the bases of the asparagus. Divide in four bundles and tie with string or elastic bands (not too tightly). Put 300ml water in the pressure cooker. Add a pinch of salt and bring to the boil. Stand the asparagus upright in the pan, resting against the sides, if necessary.

4. Cover with the lid and bring up to High pressure, then reduce the heat and cook 2 minutes only if very fresh, 3 if the asparagus has been cut a few days.

5. Remove from the heat and reduce the pressure quickly under cold water.

6. Use a sharp knife to test that the asparagus is tender. Carefully lift out the asparagus bundles and drain on kitchen paper. Cut off the string or bands from the asparagus with scissors and lay the spears on plates. Spoon the Hollandaise over the stalks. Dust the edges of the plates with paprika and serve.

This is an unusual, retro way of serving these sweet, earthy tubers. Make sure that when you peel them you put them immediately in water with a tablespoon of lemon juice added to prevent discolouration before cooking.

Serves 4 | Preparation time: 15 minutes | Cooking time: 4 minutes

Jerusalem Artichokes with Prawns

500g Jerusalem artichokes, peeled and cut into even-sized pieces

Salt and freshly ground black pepper

2 spring onions, finely chopped

2 handfuls of rocket

250g cooked, peeled cold water prawns

3 tbsp olive oil

1 tbsp lemon juice

A good pinch of caster sugar

1/2 tsp Dijon mustard

4 tbsp crème fraîche

50g jar avruga caviar or Danish lumpfish roe

To serve

Melba toast

1. Put the artichokes in the pressure cooker. Cover with water and add a pinch of salt.

2. Cover with the lid and bring up to High pressure, then reduce the heat and cook for 4 minutes.

3. Remove from the heat and reduce the pressure quickly under cold water.

4. Drain, rinse with cold water and drain again. Cut into small, neat pieces and place in a bowl with the chopped spring onion, rocket and prawns. Chill.

5. When ready to serve, blend together the oil, lemon juice, sugar, mustard and some salt and pepper. Pour over the artichoke mixture and toss gently.

6. Pile in shallow dishes, top each one with a spoonful of crème fraîche and some lumpfish roe. Serve with melba toast.

This makes a delicious starter served with some rustic bread or you could serve it for a light lunch with a large crisp salad and perhaps some new potatoes (it will then serve three people). You can use a drained can of beans and start at step 4 but add 250ml vegetable stock with them.

Serves 4–6 | Preparation time: 10 minutes, plus soaking | Cooking time: 21 minutes

Pinto Beans with Black Pudding, Dried Cranberries and Apples

100g dried pinto beans, soaked in cold water for several hours or overnight

450ml water

A handful of dried cranberries

2 tbsp red wine

2 tbsp olive oil, plus extra for garnish

1 red onion, quartered and very thinly sliced

A handful of pine nuts

2 tart eating apples, peeled, cored and diced

2 garlic cloves, crushed

150g black pudding, skinned and diced

1 tbsp finely chopped fresh rosemary

2 tbsp chopped fresh parsley

Salt and freshly ground black pepper

1. Drain the soaked beans. Put in the pressure cooker with the water. Bring to the boil in the open cooker. Skim any scum off the surface, if necessary. Reduce the heat to medium.

2. Cover with the lid and bring up to High pressure on this reduced heat, then cook for 20 minutes.

3. Remove from the heat and reduce the pressure quickly under cold water.

4. Meanwhile, soak the cranberries in the red wine for about 15 minutes.

5. Heat the oil in a small frying pan and fry the onion gently for 2 minutes to soften. Add the pine nuts and fry for 1 minute, stirring until lightly golden.

6. Add the onion mixture to the cooked beans in the pressure cooker. Also add the diced apples, garlic, black pudding, rosemary and half the parsley. Drain the cranberries and stir them in too. Season well with salt and pepper and stir gently.

7. Cover with the lid and bring up to High pressure, then reduce the heat and cook for 1 minute.

8. Remove from the heat and reduce the pressure quickly under cold water.

9. Taste and re-season. Spoon the mixture into warm bowls, drizzle with olive oil and sprinkle with the remaining parsley before serving.

A pressure cooker can make an excellent *bain marie*. Although you prepare the mixture outside the cooker, the pâté is cooked in the pressure cooker in a fraction of the time it would take in a conventional oven.

Serves 6 | Preparation time: 15 minutes | Cooking time: 20 minutes

Chicken Liver and Mushroom Pâté

125g butter, plus extra for greasing

1 small onion, quartered

1 garlic clove, roughly chopped

250g chicken livers, trimmed

1 tbsp brandy

$\frac{1}{2}$ tsp dried mixed herbs

2 tbsp double cream

Salt and freshly ground black pepper

100g button mushrooms, sliced

1 tbsp lemon juice

Mixed salad leaves and lemon wedges, to garnish

To serve

Toast

1. Melt the butter in a medium saucepan and set aside. Grease a 450g deep loaf tin or a small, deep dish and line with baking parchment.

2. With the machine running, drop the onion, garlic and chicken livers into a blender or food processor and blend until smooth, adding the brandy, herbs, about three-quarters of the butter and the cream. Season well with salt and pepper.

3. Re-heat the remaining melted butter and fry the mushrooms, stirring, for 3 minutes until tender. Stir the mushrooms and their juices into the pâté mixture. Spoon the liver mixture into the prepared tin and level the surface.

4. Cover with a double thickness of foil, twisting and folding under the rim to secure. Place in the steaming basket in the pressure cooker (it makes it easier to remove after cooking) with enough boiling water to come half way up the sides of the tin. Add the lemon juice.

5. Cover with the lid and bring up to High pressure, then reduce the heat and cook for 20 minutes.

6. Remove from the heat and allow the pressure to reduce slowly at room temperature.

7. Remove the tin from the pressure cooker. Remove the foil, re-cover with fresh foil and weigh down the top with weights or cans of food. Leave to cool, then chill.

8. When ready to serve, loosen the edge and turn out. Remove the parchment. Cut into thick slices with a sharp knife. Arrange on plates, garnish each one with a few salad leaves and a lemon wedge and serve with toast.

You can buy packs of frozen diced mixed game, which are ideal for this dish, or you can use diced venison. When fresh redcurrants are around, serve a small bunch as a garnish on the pots – it looks really pretty.

Serves 4–6 | Preparation time: 20 minutes, plus chilling | Cooking time: 45 minutes

Potted Game with Port

340g diced mixed game

2 carrots, peeled and chopped

1 onion, chopped

1 bay leaf

Freshly grated nutmeg

Salt and freshly ground black pepper

1 tbsp anchovy sauce

5 tbsp water

100g unsalted butter, diced

2 tbsp port

A few small parsley sprigs

To serve

Wholemeal toast

Mixed salad

1. Put the game in a bowl that will fit in the pressure cooker and add the carrots, onion, bay leaf, a good grating of nutmeg, a good grinding of pepper, and anchovy sauce. Add the water and butter. Cover with foil. Stand the bowl in the steamer basket in the cooker with enough boiling water to come half way up the sides of the bowl.

2. Cover with the lid and bring up to High pressure, then reduce the heat and cook for 45 minutes.

3. Remove from the heat and reduce the pressure quickly under cold water.

4. Discard the bay leaf. Tip the mixture into a food processor, add the port and run the machine until the mixture forms a smooth paste. Taste and re-season, if necessary.

5. Turn into 4–6 ramekins, or one larger pot. Cover tightly with clingfilm, leave to cool, then chill for at least 2 hours until firm. You can store it in the fridge for several days.

6. Unwrap the pots and place on plates with a tiny sprig of parsley on each or spoon the mixture out from the larger pot. Serve with wholemeal toast and a small side salad to each plate.

A 17th-century French dish, this is a predecessor to pulled pork, which is so popular today. It is a cross between potted meat and pâté and takes many hours to cook conventionally. It will keep in a sterilised jar in the fridge, well-covered in fat, for up to two weeks. Once opened, eat within two days.

Serves 4–6 | Preparation time: 5 minutes | Cooking time: 1¼ hours

Pork Rillettes

500g belly pork

2 tsp coarse sea salt

2 garlic cloves, crushed

¼ tsp ground cloves

1 large sprig of rosemary

1 large bay leaf

Freshly ground black pepper

6 tbsp water

1 tbsp lemon juice

60g lard, or goose or duck fat

To serve

Crusty French bread

Cornichons

1. Wipe the meat and rub the flesh (not the rind) all over with the salt, garlic and cloves. Place them in a bowl that will fit in the pressure cooker. Add all the remaining ingredients except the lard, or goose or duck fat. Cover with foil, twisting and folding under the rim to secure. Stand the bowl in the steamer basket in the cooker and add enough boiling water to come half way up the sides of the bowl.

2. Cover with the lid and bring up to High pressure, then reduce the heat and cook for 1¼ hours.

3. Remove from the heat and reduce the pressure quickly under cold water.

4. Lift the bowl out of the pressure cooker. Discard the herbs and leave to cool. Pull off the rind from the pork and discard any bones. Pull the meat into pieces and mince or chop in a food processor with the cooking liquid.

5. Pack into a small, clean pot, preferably with a lid. Melt the lard, or goose or duck fat and pour over the top of the meat. Cover the jar with the lid and chill until firm.

6. Serve spooned onto plates with crusty French bread and cornichons.

Chapter 8

Fish and Seafood

Fish cooks quickly, anyway, it's true, but cooking in a pressure cooker means the flesh stays moist and tender and a meal can literally be ready in minutes. It is important that you time your cooking precisely under pressure, as a minute extra can make a huge difference between perfection and overcooked fish. In many cases, the vegetable part of the dish is cooked under pressure first, then you reduce the pressure, add the fish and give a final blast to finish the dish.

When poaching fillets or whole fish, lay them on greased foil with enough at the edges to make it easy to lift them out, or on baking parchment in the steamer basket in the base of the cooker.

There are also occasions where part of the dish is pressure-cooked whilst another part is made conventionally or in the microwave. This ensures you maximise the versatility of your pressure cooker and get meals ready as quickly and efficiently as possible. It would be silly to make you do everything in the pressure cooker if it just isn't practical!

These can be served hot or cold but I prefer them cold with a crisp salad, lots of crusty bread and some unsalted butter for a delicious simple lunch or supper. You can use herring instead, if you like, but make sure you pin bone them well as they have more tiny bones than mackerel.

Serves 4 | Preparation time: 15 minutes | Cooking time: 8 minutes

Sweet Soused Mackerel with Fennel and Spring Onions

4 small mackerel, cleaned and boned

1 head of fennel, cut into fine shreds

1 bunch of spring onions, cut into short lengths then shreds

A pinch of salt

1 bay leaf

150ml white wine vinegar

150ml water

1 tbsp soft light brown sugar

6 peppercorns

1 star anise

1. Feel the fish all over and remove any remaining bones. Trim the fins and tail and open out flat. Divide the fennel and spring onion amongst the mackerel and season with a little salt. Roll up and secure with cocktail sticks.

2. Place the fish in the cooker. Cover with the vinegar, water and sugar. Tuck in the bay leaf and add the peppercorns and star anise. Lay a piece of baking parchment over the top.

3. Cover with the lid and bring up to High pressure, then reduce the heat and cook for 5 minutes.

4. Remove from the heat and reduce the pressure quickly under cold water.

5. Transfer the fish to a serving dish using a slotted spoon. Boil the liquid rapidly in the open cooker until reduced by half and slightly thickened. Pour over the fish. Serve hot or leave to cool, then chill before serving.

It's good to have a mixture of oily and white fish in this delicately flavoured stew. You can add other seafood, too, like prawns, scallops or crayfish tails, when in season. For colour, I like to throw in a handful of thawed, frozen peas for the last few minutes' cooking time.

Serves 4 | Preparation time: 10 minutes | Cooking time: 8 minutes

Saffron Fish and Baby Vegetable Stew

A large knob of butter

350g baby new potatoes, scrubbed

100g baby chantenay carrots, peeled, trimmed and washed

100g whole baby onions

100g baby corn, cut into thirds

1 bouquet garni

400ml fish or chicken stock

Salt and freshly ground black pepper

A good pinch of saffron strands

175g salmon fillet, skinned and cubed

175g meaty white fish fillet (such as haddock, cod or coley), skinned and cubed

175g smoked haddock fillet, skinned and cubed

175g raw peeled king prawns

A little chopped fresh parsley, to garnish

1. Melt the butter in the pressure cooker and fry all the vegetables, stirring, for 1 minute. Add the stock and bouquet garni. Season with salt and pepper.

2. Cover with the lid and bring up to High pressure, then reduce the heat and cook for 4 minutes.

3. Remove from the heat and reduce the pressure quickly under cold water.

4. Open the cooker and discard the bouquet garni, pressing it well against the sides of the pan to extract maximum flavour before removing. Add the saffron and all the fish. Re-cover with the lid and bring back to High pressure, then reduce the heat and cook for just 2 minutes.

5. Remove from the heat and reduce the pressure quickly under cold water.

6. Taste and re-season. Serve in bowls, garnished with chopped parsley.

For speed you can, of course, use 2 cans of borlotti beans, in which case start the recipe at the third step. You can also use other thick white fish – I often use coley for a mid-week meal as it's much cheaper (as well as being in abundance). You can also use ordinary lemon but preserved is fantastic!

Serves 4 | Preparation time: 20 minutes, plus soaking | Cooking time: 29 minutes (including beans)

Steamed Cod Loin with Roasted Pepper, Harissa and Borlotti Beans

225g dried borlotti beans, soaked in cold water for several hours or overnight

1 red pepper

2 tbsp olive oil

2 onions, finely chopped

1 garlic clove, crushed

2 carrots, peeled and finely diced

1 turnip finely diced

400g can chopped tomatoes

150ml vegetable stock

1 tsp dried oregano

2 tbsp tomato purée

4 pieces of cod loin, about 150g each, skinned, if liked

4 tsp harissa paste

1 preserved lemon, cut into 8 slices

Salt and freshly ground black pepper

A few torn coriander leaves, to garnish

To serve

Crusty bread

Green salad

1. Drain the beans and place in the cooker. Cover with plenty of cold water but make sure the cooker is not more than one-third full. Bring to the boil in the open cooker. Skim, then reduce the heat to medium.

2. Cover with the lid and bring up to High pressure over a medium heat, then cook for 20 minutes.

3. Meanwhile, put the pepper on a skewer and roast over a gas flame, or place under a hot grill and cook, turning occasionally, until blackened all over. Place in a plastic bag and leave until cool enough to handle, then scrape off the black skin, remove the stalk and seeds, rinse, drain, and dice.

4. Remove the pressure cooker from the heat and reduce the pressure quickly under cold water. Drain and reserve the beans, then rinse out and dry the pressure cooker.

5. Heat the olive oil in the cooker. Add the onion, garlic, carrot and turnip and fry gently, stirring, for 3 minutes until softened but not browned. Stir in the tomatoes, stock and oregano.

6. Cover with the lid and bring up to High pressure, then reduce the heat and cook for 3 minutes.

7. Remove from the heat and reduce the pressure quickly under cold water.

8. Stir in the tomato purée, red pepper and the beans. Smear the fish with the harissa paste and lay it on top of the bean mixture. Lay 2 lemon slices on top of each piece of fish. Season with salt and pepper, cover with the lid and bring back to High pressure, then reduce the heat and cook for 3 minutes.

9. Remove from the heat and reduce the pressure quickly under cold water.

10. Serve the fish and vegetables garnished with torn coriander and with crusty bread and a green salad.

This has a lovely Mediterranean feel to it. The meaty fish with the fruity yet salty-flavoured sauce is perfect for a late summer meal. Monkfish comes into season in August, so look out for it. Use streaky bacon if pancetta is not available.

Serves 4 | Preparation time: 15 minutes | Cooking time: 14–15 minutes

Monkfish with Tomato and Caperberry Sauce and Crispy Pancetta

2 tbsp olive oil

1 large onion, finely chopped

1 head of fennel, thinly sliced

1 large garlic clove, crushed

3 beefsteak tomatoes, skinned and chopped

150ml dry white wine

100ml fish or chicken stock

2 tbsp tomato purée

A large pinch of caster sugar

1 tbsp fresh chopped thyme plus extra leaves to garnish

4 small thick pieces of monkfish fillet, about 150g each

50g black olives, stoned

30g drained pickled caperberries

Salt and freshly ground black pepper

4 thin slices of pancetta

To serve

Couscous

Green salad

1. Heat the oil in the pressure cooker, add the onion, fennel and garlic and fry gently, stirring, for 5 minutes until softened but not browned. Add the tomatoes, wine, stock, tomato purée, sugar and herbs.

2. Cover with the lid and bring up to High pressure, then reduce the heat and cook for 3 minutes.

3. Remove from the heat and reduce the pressure quickly under cold water.

4. Lay the fish on top of the tomatoes, scatter the olives and caperberries over the top and season lightly with salt and pepper. Bring back to pressure and cook for 3 minutes.

5. Remove from the heat and reduce the pressure quickly under cold water.

6. Meanwhile, grill or fry the pancetta until crisp. Carefully lift the fish out of the cooker and keep it warm. Boil the remaining contents of the pressure cooker rapidly for 3–4 minutes, stirring, to reduce by about half.

7. Serve the fish and sauce on a bed of couscous, top each one with a piece of crispy pancetta, and accompany with a green salad.

I've cooked new potatoes in the base of the pan to serve with the fish but you can cook them separately if you prefer. This is also great with oily fish like mackerel, or even thick salmon fillets.

Serves 4 | Preparation time: 25 minutes | Cooking time: 5 minutes

Red Mullet Parcels with Rosemary, Peppers and Courgettes

400g baby new potatoes, scrubbed

Salt and freshly ground black pepper

1 sprig of fresh mint

2 tbsp olive oil

1 courgette, thinly sliced

1 red pepper, thinly sliced

1 yellow pepper, thinly sliced

4 small red mullet, cleaned and de-scaled

2 tbsp chopped fresh rosemary

50g can anchovy fillets, drained

2 tbsp chopped fresh parsley, plus extra for garnish

4 tbsp medium sweet cider or apple juice

4 tbsp water

1. Put the potatoes in the pressure cooker. Add a large pinch of salt and the mint and just cover with water.

2. Cut four large pieces of foil about 30x40cm and brush them with olive oil. Spread the courgettes and peppers in a single layer in the centre of each piece of foil as a base for the fish, leaving plenty of foil free round the edges. Sprinkle with the rosemary. Lay the fish on the vegetables. Lay the anchovies over, then sprinkle with the parsley. Add a very little salt and a good grinding of black pepper. Spoon a tablespoon of cider or apple juice and a tablespoon of water over each. Draw the foil up over the fish and fold over the top and sides to form sealed parcels.

3. Place two parcels one way in the steamer basket and two at right angles on top. Lay the basket on top of the potatoes in the pressure cooker.

4. Cover with the lid and bring up to High pressure, then reduce the heat and cook for 5 minutes.

5. Remove from the heat and reduce the pressure quickly under cold water.

6. Carefully lift the fish parcels out of the cooker. Drain the potatoes, place in a serving dish and sprinkle with a little parsley. Put the fish parcels on plates and open at the table so you get the full, delicious aroma from them. Serve with the potatoes.

This classic cooks really quickly with the help of the pressure cooker. You still need to brown the top but that can be done under the grill rather than in the oven to save on fuel. If you prefer to finish the top in the oven, preheat the oven to 190°C/gas 5 and bake for about 30 minutes instead.

Serves 4 | Preparation time: 20 minutes | Cooking time: 16 minutes

Fish Pie

1kg potatoes, peeled and cut into small chunks

Salt and freshly ground black pepper

40g butter

300ml milk

1 onion, chopped

1 carrot, peeled and sliced

1 bay leaf

700g white fish fillet (coley or pollack is fine), skinned

100g button mushrooms, sliced

100g frozen peas

3–4 tbsp plain flour

3–4 tbsp water

2 hard-boiled eggs, quartered (optional)

A small handful of chopped fresh parsley

Freshly grated nutmeg

1. Put the potatoes in the pressure cooker, just cover with water and add a large pinch of salt.

2. Cover with the lid and bring up to High pressure, then reduce the heat and cook for 4 minutes.

3. Remove from the heat and reduce the pressure quickly under cold water.

4. Drain, tip into a bowl and mash well with about a quarter of the butter and a splash of the milk. Rinse out and dry the pressure cooker.

5. Melt half the remaining butter in the pressure cooker. Add the onion and carrot and fry, stirring, for 3 minutes until softening but not browned. Add the remaining milk, fish, bay leaf, mushrooms and peas.

6. Cover with the lid and bring up to High pressure over a medium heat (so the milk doesn't foam up), and cook for 4 minutes.

7. Remove from the heat and allow the pressure to reduce slowly at room temperature.

8. Carefully lift the fish out of the cooker onto a plate using a slotted spoon. Blend the flour with the water and stir into the cooking liquid. Bring to the boil in the open cooker and cook, stirring, for 2 minutes until thickened to your liking. Discard the bay leaf. Season to taste with salt and pepper.

9. Preheat the grill. Flake the fish and place in a 1.2 litre flameproof serving dish. Add the eggs, if using, and the sauce and mix gently. Spoon the potato over the top and rough up with a fork. Dot with the remaining butter. Place under the hot grill and cook for about 6 minutes until golden on top. Serve hot.

This deconstructed pie is so quick to make. Yes, you do have to put the oven on briefly but for far less time than if you were cooking a whole pie conventionally. Use it to warm the plates too. You must use double cream as you are boiling it, and any other will curdle.

Serves 4 | Preparation time: 10 minutes | Cooking time: 6 minutes

Seafood in Creamy White Wine Sauce with Crispy Filo Top

150ml fruity white wine

1 bunch of spring onions, chopped

1 bouquet garni

400g mixed raw seafood, thawed if frozen

200g salmon fillet, skinned and cubed

150ml double cream

2 tbsp cornflour

2 tbsp milk

Salt and freshly ground black pepper

2 tbsp chopped fresh parsley

1 tsp Thai fish sauce

For the topping

4 sheets of filo pastry

15g butter

To serve

Green beans

1. Preheat the oven to 200°C/gas 6.

2. Put the wine, spring onions and bouquet garni in the pressure cooker. Boil for 3 minutes until reduced by half. Stir in the seafood, salmon and cream. Reduce the heat to medium.

3. Cover with the lid and bring up to High pressure over this medium heat, then cook for 2 minutes.

4. Remove from the heat and reduce the pressure quickly under cold water.

5. Meanwhile, brush the filo sheets with the melted butter. Scrunch each sheet as if scrunching a piece of paper and place on a baking sheet. Bake for 5 minutes until crisp and golden.

6. Blend the cornflour with the water and stir into the seafood. Bring to the boil, stirring, and cook for 1 minute until thickened.

7. Discard the bouquet garni and season to taste with salt and pepper. Stir in the parsley. Spoon the seafood and sauce on plates and top with the crispy filo. Serve with green beans.

You can't cook more than 1kg of mussels at a time in the pressure cooker otherwise there will be no room for them when they open. If you want to cook more, remove the first batch with a slotted spoon, then quickly cook another batch.

Serves 4 | Preparation time: 25 minutes | Cooking time: 4 minutes

Mussels with Cream, Pernod and Fennel

1kg fresh mussels in their shells

A knob of butter

2 shallots, finely chopped

1 garlic clove, finely chopped

1 carrot, peeled and finely chopped

1 head of fennel, green fronds trimmed and reserved, then finely chopped

2 star anise

120ml dry white wine

90ml water

3 tbsp Pernod

Freshly ground black pepper

6 tbsp double cream

A handful of chopped fresh parsley

To serve

Crusty bread

1. Scrub the mussels and pull off the beards attached to the shell. Discard any that are broken or open and don't close when tapped sharply with a knife.

2. Heat the butter in the pressure cooker. Add the shallots, garlic, carrot and fennel and cook very gently in the covered pan for 3 minutes to soften but do not allow to brown. Add the star anise, mussels, wine, water, Pernod and some freshly ground black pepper.

3. Cover with the lid and bring just up to High pressure, then reduce the heat and release the pressure immediately under cold water.

4. Transfer the mussels to large bowls using a slotted spoon, discarding the star anise and any mussels that have remained closed. Stir the cream into the liquid in the cooker and reheat. Spoon over the mussels and sprinkle with chopped parsley. Serve straight away with plenty of crusty bread to mop up the juices.

Pasta is fine cooked in the pressure cooker as long as you time it properly. Here you quickly steam the clams first, then cook the pasta in the juices and return the seafood at the last minute.

Serves 4 | Preparation time: 15 minutes | Cooking time: 6 minutes

Macaroni with Chorizo and Clams

A knob of butter

1 leek, chopped

1 large garlic clove, crushed

250ml dry white wine

300ml water

1kg fresh clams, scrubbed

350g macaroni

$\frac{1}{2}$ tsp ground turmeric

$\frac{1}{2}$ tsp sweet paprika

150g diced chorizo

100g fresh shelled or frozen soya beans

1 tbsp chopped fresh thyme

Salt and freshly ground black pepper

Handful of chopped parsley

To garnish

1 lemon, cut into wedges

1. Melt the butter in the pressure cooker. Add the leek and garlic and fry, stirring, for 2 minutes. Add the wine, water and clams.

2. Cover with the lid and bring up to High pressure, then immediately reduce the pressure quickly under cold water.

3. Discard any clams that have not opened. Remove all the clams from the cooker with a slotted spoon and set aside.

4. Bring back to the boil, add the macaroni, spices, chorizo, soya beans and thyme to the liquid. Season with salt and pepper and stir well.

5. Cover with the lid and bring up to High pressure over a medium heat, then cook for 4 minutes.

6. Remove from the heat and allow the pressure to reduce slowly at room temperature.

7. Taste and re-season. Stir the clams and parsley through the pasta and re-heat briefly. Serve in bowls, garnished with the lemon wedges.

This is a one-pot meal cooked in minutes. Try it with salmon or white fish instead of smoked haddock but add a teaspoon of curry powder to the rice.

Serves 4 | Preparation time: 10 minutes | Cooking time: 10 minutes

Kedgeree

2 eggs, scrubbed under cold water

A knob of butter

1 onion, chopped

225g long-grain rice

500ml boiling chicken or fish stock

100g frozen peas

350g smoked haddock fillet, skinned

A handful of chopped fresh parsley

2 tbsp single cream

Freshly grated nutmeg

Salt and freshly ground black pepper

1. Wrap the eggs in foil. Place in a non-perforated separator if your pressure cooker has one, or use a small bowl.

2. Melt the butter in the pressure cooker. Add the onion and fry, stirring, for 3 minutes until lightly golden. Stir in the rice until glistening. Push the rice away from one side of the cooker and stand the container with the eggs in the gap. Pour the stock over the rice, add the peas, stir, then put the fish on top.

3. Cover with the lid and bring up to High pressure over a medium heat, then cook for 3 minutes.

4. Remove from the heat and allow the pressure to reduce slowly at room temperature.

5. Lift the bowl with the eggs out of the cooker and cover immediately with cold water.

6. Flake the fish, then stir into the mixture and re-cover the pan.

7. Shell the eggs and cut into quarters. Stir half the parsley and all the cream into the rice, season with nutmeg, salt and pepper. Heat through briefly. Spoon into bowls and top with the egg quarters and sprinkle with the remaining parsley before serving.

Chapter 9

Beef and Lamb

Using a pressure cooker means you can often use cheaper cuts of meat as they tenderise beautifully without the need for the long, slow cooking that is needed to tenderise meat in the conventional oven.

But you don't have to use the pressure cooker only for stews and casseroles. There are numerous recipes here for cooking joints, meat for pies and other classic dishes that will save you time and energy if you cook them in the pressure cooker but ensure delicious and tender results.

For some of the recipes, you will be using your cooker for a complete meal, for others it will be a vital part of the preparation and then you will be finishing off by a more conventional method. It's all about learning to make your cooker work for you in your kitchen.

This is my quick version of Boeuf Bourguignon that normally takes at least 2 hours in the oven. Here it's cooked in just 20 minutes and with very little preparation! Traditionally it's made with baby whole onions, but I've used chopped – it doesn't make a lot of difference to the flavour but is much quicker to do.

Serves 4 | Preparation time: 10 minutes | Cooking time: 20 minutes

Beef and Mushrooms in Red Wine

2 tbsp olive oil

1 large onion, chopped (or 2 large handfuls frozen chopped onion)

75g diced pancetta

675g lean diced braising steak

1 garlic clove, crushed

16 baby chantenay carrots, peeled and topped and tailed

100g button mushrooms

1 tbsp brandy

200ml red wine

150ml beef stock

1 tbsp tomato purée

A large pinch of caster sugar

1 bouquet garni sachet

Salt and freshly ground black pepper

3 tbsp plain flour

3 tbsp water

To serve

Fluffy mashed potatoes

Green beans

1. Heat the oil in the pressure cooker and fry the onion and pancetta for 3 minutes, stirring. Add the meat and brown on all sides. Stir in the garlic, carrots and mushrooms. Add the brandy, wine, stock and tomato purée. Bring to the boil, stirring until thickened. Stir in the sugar, bouquet garni and some salt and pepper.

2. Cover with the lid and bring up to High pressure over a medium heat, then reduce the heat and cook for 20 minutes.

3. Remove from the heat and reduce the pressure quickly under cold water.

4. Discard the bouquet garni. Blend the flour and water together and stir into the pan. Bring to the boil and cook for 2 minutes, stirring until thickened.

5. Taste and re-season, if necessary. Serve hot with fluffy mash and green beans.

Cooking the meat in the pressure cooker saves a huge amount of time when you want to make pies. You can make individual pies if you prefer; they'll take a little less time to brown in the oven. For steak and kidney, replace 225g beef with ox kidney.

Serves 4 | Preparation time: 30 minutes | Cooking time: 40 minutes

Steak and Ale Pie

1 tbsp sunflower oil

1 onion, chopped

700g lean stewing steak, cut into dice

200g baby button mushrooms

200ml beef stock

200ml brown ale or stout

1 tbsp soy sauce

Salt and freshly ground black pepper

1 bay leaf

5 tbsp plain flour

5 tbsp water

350g ready-made puff pastry, thawed if frozen

Beaten egg, to glaze

To serve

Mashed potatoes

Peas and carrots

1. Heat the oil in the pressure cooker. Add the onion and meat and fry for 3 minutes, stirring, until lightly golden. Add the mushrooms, stock, brown ale, soy sauce, a little seasoning and the bay leaf.

2. Cover with the lid and bring up to High pressure, then reduce the heat and cook for 20 minutes.

3. Remove from the heat and reduce the pressure quickly under cold water.

4. Blend the flour with the water and stir into the meat in the open cooker. Simmer, stirring, for 2 minutes until thickened. Transfer the meat mixture to a large pie dish using a slotted spoon. Put a pie funnel in the centre, if you like. Moisten the meat with as much of the gravy as you like (reserve the remainder to heat and serve separately).

5. Preheat the oven to 200°C/gas 6.

6. Roll out the pastry slightly larger than the pie dish. Cut a strip of pastry to go round the rim, dampen it with water and press the pastry in place. Brush with water. Lay the pastry lid in place. Press the edges together to seal and flute with the back of a knife. Make a slit in the centre to allow steam to escape. Use trimmings to decorate the pie, if liked. Transfer to a baking sheet.

7. Brush the pastry with beaten egg to glaze. Bake in the oven for 30–40 minutes or until puffy and golden brown.

8. Serve the pie with mashed potatoes, peas and carrots.

For those of you who adore Yorkshire puddings, use ready-made ones and pop them in the oven to heat through just before the meat is ready. This recipe gives beef that is still pink in the middle, for well-done meat, cook about 5 minutes longer.

Serves 4 | Preparation time: 10 minutes | Cooking time: 30 minutes

Pot Roast Beef with Parsnips, Baby Carrots with Sweet Mustard Relish

700g piece of topside or top rump of beef

Salt and freshly ground black pepper

A knob of butter

1 tbsp sunflower oil

200g baby chantenay carrots, peeled and topped and tailed

I large parsnip, halved widthways and cut into chunky sticks

350g baby new potatoes, scrubbed

1 tbsp fresh chopped thyme

1 bay leaf

300ml beef stock

2 tbsp plain flour

4 tbsp water

2 tsp soy sauce

For the relish

4 tbsp crème fraîche

1 tsp English mustard

1½ tsp clear honey

1½ tsp white wine vinegar

To serve

Shredded greens

1. Season the beef with salt and pepper. Heat the butter and oil in the pressure cooker, add the beef and brown on all sides. Remove the meat from the cooker. Add the vegetables and fry, stirring, for 1 minute. Season lightly with salt and pepper. Return the beef to the pan, sprinkle with the thyme and add the bay leaf and stock.

2. Cover with the lid, bring up to High pressure, then reduce the heat and cook for 20 minutes.

3. Remove from the heat and reduce the pressure quickly under cold water.

4. Meanwhile, mix the relish ingredients together in a small bowl. Season to taste with salt and pepper. Chill until ready to serve.

5. Use a slotted spoon to transfer the meat to a carving dish and the vegetables to a serving dish. Keep them warm.

6. Blend together the flour, water and soy sauce and stir into the liquid in the pressure cooker. Bring to the boil and cook for 2 minutes, stirring.

7. Season to taste. Carve the meat and serve with the vegetables, greens, the gravy and relish.

This is so simple and can be made in an open cooker with expensive rump steak but, using cheaper braising steak, it takes just minutes to become meltingly tender in the pressure cooker. Tossing the meat in cornflour helps prevent the coconut milk from 'splitting' during cooking.

Serves 4 | Preparation time: 10 minutes | Cooking time: 30 minutes

Thai Red Beef and Pepper Curry

600g braising steak, cut into large cubes

2 tbsp cornflour

2 tbsp sunflower oil

2 garlic cloves, crushed

1 bunch of spring onions, cut into short lengths

2 large potatoes, peeled and cut into fairly large chunks

2 red peppers, cut into chunks

4 tbsp Thai red curry paste

1 tsp grated fresh root ginger

400g can of coconut milk

1 tbsp Thai fish sauce

2 thin red chillies, deseeded and cut into thin strips

Salt and freshly ground black pepper

50g raw cashew nuts

4 tomatoes, quartered

To garnish

A small handful of coriander leaves, torn

1 lime, cut into wedges

To serve

Thai Jasmine rice

1. Toss the meat in the cornflour. Heat the oil in the pressure cooker, add the garlic, spring onions and meat and cook, stirring and turning, for about 3 minutes until the meat is browned. Add the potatoes and peppers. Blend the curry paste with the ginger, coconut milk and fish sauce and add to the pan. Scatter the chilli strips over the top.

2. Cover with the lid and bring up to High pressure, then reduce the heat and cook for 20 minutes.

3. Remove from the heat and reduce the pressure quickly under cold water.

4. Gently stir in the nuts and tomatoes. Re-cover and leave for 5 minutes.

5. Serve spooned over Jasmine rice in bowls and garnish each bowl with a scattering of coriander leaves and a lime wedge.

There are so many recipes for this traditional Moroccan dish but I've made it as simple as possible. Use 100g dried chickpeas if preferred, simply cook them as on the chart p23 then continue as in the recipe here. Lamb can be used instead of beef too.

Serves 4 | Preparation time: 10 minutes | Cooking time: 35 minutes

Moroccan-style Couscous with Beef

2 tbsp olive oil

2 large onions, chopped

500g braising steak, cut into large chunks

400g can of chickpeas, drained

1 tsp ground ginger

1 tsp sweet paprika

¼ tsp cayenne

½ tsp ground cumin

1 tsp ground cinnamon

1 tsp clear honey

500ml beef stock

1 tbsp tomato purée

Salt and freshly ground black pepper

250g baby chantenay carrots, peeled and trimmed

2 turnips, cut into chunks

4 tomatoes, skinned and chopped

2 large courgettes, cut into chunks

100g green beans, topped, tailed and halved

½ small white cabbage, cut into wedges

225g couscous

Chopped fresh coriander, to garnish

1. Heat the oil in the pressure cooker. Add the onions and fry, stirring, for 2 minutes. Remove with a slotted spoon and set aside. Add the beef and brown all over in the pan. Add the drained chickpeas, the onions, the spices, honey, 250ml of the stock, and the tomatoe purée. Season with salt and pepper.

2. Cover with the lid and bring up to High pressure, then reduce the heat and cook for 25 minutes.

3. Remove from the heat and allow the pressure to reduce slowly at room temperature.

4. When the pressure is reduced, add all the vegetables. Bring back to High pressure, reduce the heat and cook for 4 minutes.

5. Remove from the heat and reduce the pressure quickly under cold water.

6. Meanwhile, put the couscous in a bowl, heat the remaining stock until boiling and pour over the couscous. Leave to stand for 5 minutes, then fluff up with a fork. Taste the meat mixture and re-season as necessary.

7. Pile the couscous onto warm serving plates and make a well in the centre. Lift out the meat and vegetables with a slotted spoon and pile in the centre. Garnish with coriander and serve the juices separately.

I've used braising steak, cut into small dice, rather than the more usual mince as it gives such a delicious, meaty flavour and cooking it in the pressure cooker is still quicker than cooking with mince conventionally.

Serves 4 | Preparation time: 15 minutes | Cooking time: 15 minutes

Chunky Chilli con Carne

1 tbsp sunflower oil

500g lean braising steak, cut into 1cm cubes

1 large onion, chopped

1 green pepper, chopped

1 large garlic clove, crushed

400g can of chopped tomatoes

1 tbsp tomato purée

3 tbsp chopped pickled jalapeño peppers

½-1 tsp chilli powder (according to taste)

1 tsp ground cumin

1 tsp dried oregano

1 tsp caster sugar

2 x 400g cans red kidney beans, drained and rinsed

150ml beef stock

Salt and freshly ground black pepper

For the guacamole

2 avocados

1 tbsp lime juice

1 tbsp chopped fresh coriander

To serve

Grated cheese, shredded lettuce, finely chopped onion, and corn tortilla chips

1. Heat the oil in the pressure cooker. Add the beef and the onion, and fry, stirring, until the meat is browned all over. Add all the remaining ingredients and stir well.

2. Cover with the lid and bring up to High pressure, then reduce the heat and cook for 15 minutes.

3. Remove from the heat and reduce the pressure quickly under cold water.

4. Return the pan to the heat and boil the mixture rapidly in the open pan for a few minutes until rich and thick, stirring frequently. Taste and re-season, if necessary.

5. Meanwhile, mash the avocados with the lime juice. Season lightly with salt and pepper. Stir in the chopped coriander.

6. Serve the chilli with the guacamole, grated cheese, finely chopped onion and corn tortilla chips.

I like to cook the pasta while I make the sauce, then it's all ready together. Use the same meat sauce to make a lasagne. Simply layer the meat with lasagne sheets, top with béchamel or cheese sauce and bake in a hot oven at 200°C/gas 6 for about 35 minutes.

Serves 4 | Preparation time: 5 minutes | Cooking time: 15 minutes

Spaghetti Bolognese

2 tbsp olive oil

1 onion, chopped

1 garlic clove, crushed

1 large carrot, peeled and finely diced

450g lean minced beef

400g can chopped tomatoes

2 tbsp tomato purée

150ml beef stock

1 tsp dried oregano

1 slice lemon

1 bay leaf

A large pinch of caster sugar

Salt and freshly ground black pepper

350–450g spaghetti depending on appetites

Freshly grated Parmesan cheese

1. Heat the oil in the pressure cooker and fry the onion, garlic, carrot and beef, stirring, until the beef is no longer pink and all the minced grains are separate. Add all the remaining ingredients except the spaghetti and Parmesan.

2. Cover with the lid and bring up to High pressure, then reduce the heat and cook for 10 minutes.

3. Remove from the heat and reduce the pressure quickly under cold water.

4. Return to the heat and boil the mixture in the open cooker for a few minutes to reduce the liquid and thicken slightly. Taste, re-season, and discard the lemon and bay leaf.

5. Meanwhile, cook the spaghetti according to the packet directions. Drain.

6. Pile the spaghetti into pasta bowls, top with the bolognese and sprinkle with grated Parmesan to serve.

This is one of my favourite Mexican dishes: a mixture of rich meat, salt, olives, hot chilli and sweet raisins, topped off with fried eggs. It's perfect with rolled up flour tortillas to eat with it instead of bread. It works a dream in the pressure cooker.

Serves 4 | Preparation time: 15 minutes | Cooking time: 22 minutes

Picadillo

700g lean braising steak, cut into large cubes

Salt and freshly ground black pepper

Sunflower oil, for frying

1 large onion, finely chopped

1 large garlic clove, finely chopped

2 large green peppers, finely chopped

1 green chilli, seeded and finely chopped

A large pinch of ground cloves

4 large tomatoes, skinned and chopped

1 tbsp tomato purée

½ tsp caster sugar

75g stuffed green olives, halved

50g raisins

2 tsp balsamic vinegar

2 tbsp chopped fresh coriander

4 eggs

1. Put the beef in the pressure cooker, just cover with water, add a pinch of salt and plenty of freshly ground black pepper. Bring to the boil and skim any scum from the surface.

2. Cover with the lid and bring up to High pressure, then reduce the heat and cook for 20 minutes until really tender.

3. Remove from the heat and reduce the pressure quickly under cold water.

4. Meanwhile, heat 2 tbsp sunflower oil in a saucepan. Add the onion and fry, stirring, for 5 minutes. Add all the remaining ingredients except the coriander and eggs. Bring to the boil and boil rapidly for about 5 minutes, stirring occasionally, until thick and pulpy. Season to taste with salt and pepper.

5. When the beef is cooked, drain it well, reserving the stock for soup. Chop the meat, which should fall apart easily. Stir the meat into the tomato mixture. Taste and re-season, as necessary. Heat through gently.

6. Heat enough oil to cover the base of a large frying pan and fry the eggs to your liking, basting with the oil, if liked.

7. Spoon the beef mixture into shallow bowls, sprinkle with coriander and top with the eggs to serve.

Timing is important with lamb shanks. If you cook them for too long they will, literally, fall off the bones – not attractive – and as they are quite expensive, you want them meltingly tender but whole. To prevent them from going brown, put the prepared celeriac and potatoes in water with 1 tbsp lemon juice until you are ready to cook.

Serves 4 | Preparation time: 25 minutes | Cooking time: 55 minutes

Lamb Shanks in Pink Peppercorn Sauce with Celeriac and Potato Garlic Mash

1 tbsp sunflower oil

4 lamb shanks

2 tbsp redcurrant jelly, warmed

2-3 tbsp coarsely crushed pink peppercorns

250ml lamb or chicken stock

4 tbsp red wine

Salt and freshly ground black pepper

1 tbsp chopped fresh rosemary, plus 4 small sprigs to garnish

2 tbsp cornflour

2 tbsp water

For the celeriac and potato garlic mash

1 small celeriac, peeled and cut into small chunks

500g potatoes, peeled and cut into small chunks

2 garlic cloves, chopped

15g butter

2 tbsp double cream

To serve

Broccoli

1. Heat the oil in the open cooker, add the lamb and brown on all sides. Lift them out of the cooker, brush with some of the jelly and coat in the crushed peppercorns.

2. Wipe out the cooker and stir in the stock, wine and remaining jelly, mix well, then return the shanks to the pan. Season with salt and pepper and sprinkle with the rosemary.

3. Cover with the lid and bring up to High pressure, then reduce the heat and cook for 50 minutes.

4. Remove from the heat and reduce the pressure quickly under cold water.

5. Lift out the lamb and keep it warm. Put the celeriac and potatoes in the steamer basket. Place the trivet in the liquid in the pan and put the basket on top. Sprinkle the vegetables with the chopped garlic and a little salt.

6. Cover with the lid, bring back to High pressure over a medium heat, then cook for 5 minutes.

7. Remove from the heat and reduce the pressure quickly under cold water.

8. Tip the potatoes and celeriac into a bowl. Mash well with half the butter and the cream. Season to taste and keep warm. Remove the trivet from the cooker.

9. Blend the cornflour with the water and stir into the liquid in the pan. Bring to the boil and cook for 1 minute, stirring, until thickened. Taste and re-season, if necessary.

10. Pile the mash on four plates. Lay a lamb shank on each one and spoon the sauce over. Garnish each one with a tiny sprig of rosemary and serve with broccoli.

This is rich and nourishing on a chilly day. It's a complete meal so makes washing up really easy! Stewing lamb chops contain a lot of bone but this adds wonderful flavour and is relatively inexpensive. Use boneless diced lamb, if you prefer, but reduce the quantity to 500g.

Serves 4 | Preparation time: 10 minutes | Cooking time: 30 minutes

Lamb, Leek and Cabbage Stew with Rosemary Dumplings

700g stewing lamb neck chops

1 tbsp pickled capers

2 leeks, trimmed and cut into thick chunks

500g small waxy potatoes, scrubbed

1 small white cabbage, cored and cut into chunks

4 carrots, peeled and thickly sliced

Salt and freshly ground black pepper

1 bay leaf

450ml lamb stock

For the dumplings

100g self-raising flour

A large pinch of salt

40g butter, cut into small pieces

1 tbsp chopped fresh rosemary

2 tbsp chopped fresh parsley

4 tbsp cold water to mix

1. Put all the stew ingredients in the pressure cooker.

2. Cover with the lid and bring up to High pressure, then reduce the heat and cook for 15 minutes.

3. Meanwhile, make the dumplings. Put the flour and salt in a bowl. Add the butter and rub in with the fingertips until the mixture resembles breadcrumbs. Stir in the rosemary and half the parsley. Mix with enough cold water to form a soft but not too sticky dough. Quickly shape into 8 small balls.

4. Remove the pressure cooker from the heat and reduce the pressure quickly under cold water.

5. Open the pressure cooker. Discard the bay leaf. Put the dumplings round the edge of the stew. Cover and simmer gently without pressure for 15 minutes until the dumplings are fluffy and cooked through. Serve straight away.

This is an inexpensive cut and worth seeking out. If you can't find a breast of lamb, buy a small boned shoulder and treat it in the same way. I cook the greens separately – they only take a few minutes – whilst the lamb is resting and the sauce is thickening.

Serves 4 | Preparation time: 20 minutes | Cooking time: 20 minutes

Stuffed Breast of Lamb Noisettes

175g fresh white breadcrumbs

1 tbsp chopped fresh parsley

1 tbsp chopped fresh rosemary

2 tbsp currants

Finely grated zest of ½ lemon

Salt and freshly ground black pepper

1 egg, beaten

1 breast of lamb, boned and excess fat trimmed off

A knob of butter

450ml lamb or chicken stock

12–16 small waxy potatoes, scrubbed

2 tbsp redcurrant jelly

2 tbsp plain flour

2 tsp cold water

1 tbsp soy sauce

To serve

Wilted spinach

1. Mix the breadcrumbs with the herbs, currants, lemon zest and plenty of salt and pepper. Add the beaten egg to bind. Open out the trimmed lamb breast and spread the stuffing over. Roll up and tie securely at four even intervals. Cut into four thick noisettes between each piece of string (so each one is tied securely).

2. Heat the butter in the pressure cooker and fry the noisettes quickly on both sides to brown, then remove them from the pan and place in the steaming basket. Drain off any remaining fat in the pan. Add the trivet and pour in the stock. Arrange the potatoes in the pan. Put the basket on the trivet.

3. Cover with the lid and bring up to High pressure, then reduce the heat and cook for 15 minutes.

4. Remove from the heat and reduce the pressure quickly under cold water.

5. Lift out the lamb and keep it warm. Remove the trivet. Lift out the potatoes with a draining spoon and keep them warm. Stir the redcurrant jelly into the stock until melted. Blend the flour with the water and soy sauce until smooth, then stir into the stock. Bring to the boil and cook for 2 minutes, stirring. Taste and re-season, if necessary. Serve the lamb and the potatoes on a bed of wilted spinach with the sauce spooned over.

A tagine is an earthenware pot used to cook stews over charcoal, but the Middle Eastern flavours can be replicated quickly and effectively in a pressure cooker. I always add a little smoked paprika to add a slightly smoky edge.

Serves 4 | Preparation time: 10 minutes | Cooking time: 20 minutes

Lamb Tagine with Apricots

600ml boiling lamb stock

700g lean diced lamb

12 button onions, peeled but left whole

2 courgettes, diced

2 carrots, peeled and diced

1 green pepper, diced

100g ready-to-eat dried apricots, halved

1 large garlic clove, crushed

$\frac{1}{2}$ tsp ground cinnamon

$\frac{1}{2}$ tsp ground ginger

$\frac{1}{2}$ tsp smoked paprika

Salt and freshly ground black pepper

2 tbsp tomato purée

2 tbsp chopped fresh coriander

2 tbsp chopped fresh mint

225g couscous

To serve

Mixed salad

1. Put 350ml of the stock in the pressure cooker with all the remaining ingredients except the herbs and couscous.

2. Cover with the lid and bring up to High pressure, then reduce the heat and cook for 12 minutes.

3. Remove from the heat and reduce the pressure quickly under cold water.

4. Meanwhile, put the couscous in a shallow heatproof bowl that will fit in the pressure cooker. Add the remaining stock. Stir well and leave to soak.

5. Open the pressure cooker and stir in half the herbs. Rest the bowl of couscous on top.

6. Cover with the lid, bring back to pressure and cook for 3 minutes.

7. Remove from the heat and reduce the pressure quickly under cold water.

8. Lift out the couscous and fluff up with a fork. Taste the tagine and re-season, if necessary.

9. Spoon the couscous onto serving plates. Spoon the lamb mixture on top and sprinkle with the remaining herbs before serving with a mixed salad.

Chapter 10

Pork

When pork is cooked conventionally, it can sometimes go dry but in the pressure cooker, it retains all its moisture and succulence. If you are cooking a joint, make sure the size is right for the cooker as you should never fill your pressure cooker too full. Make sure you trim off any excess fat before cooking, particularly if you are going to use the cooking liquid for a sauce (except for Rillettes, where it is a vital part of the dish). Having said that, however, I find that it isn't always necessary as these days the meat tends to be leaner than it used to be.

You can get quite a lot of sticky spare rib recipes but I prefer this dryer version, which is packed with flavour. Pressure cooking the ribs first makes them meltingly tender – fast!

Serves 4 | Preparation time: 5 minutes | Cooking time: 30 minutes

Chinese-style Spare Ribs

900g Chinese short spare ribs

1 tbsp white wine vinegar

2 tbsp sunflower oil

1 tsp sesame oil

2 tsp grated fresh root ginger

2 garlic cloves, crushed

3 tbsp clear honey

2 tsp Chinese five-spice powder

¼ tsp chilli powder

5 tbsp soy sauce

1. Put the ribs in the pressure cooker, just cover with water and add the vinegar.

2. Cover with the lid, bring up to High pressure, then reduce the heat and cook for 15 minutes.

3. Remove from the heat and reduce the pressure quickly under cold water.

4. Drain the ribs thoroughly, then tip them back into the cooker.

5. Preheat the grill and line the grill pan with foil. Mix all the remaining ingredients together, pour over the ribs and toss well to coat completely.

6. Arrange the ribs in a single layer in the grill pan and set it about 5cm from the heat source. Grill, turning occasionally, for 12–15 minutes until well-browned all over and glazed, brushing with any remaining marinade during cooking. Serve hot.

This recipe originally comes from Goa, an island off Southern India. I've added my own touches to make it fiery and rich. It traditionally uses malt vinegar but I like the mellow flavour of balsamic, while the addition of potatoes lifts it too.

Serves 4 | Preparation time: 10 minutes | Cooking time: 25 minutes

Hot Pork Liver and Potato Curry

2 tbsp sunflower oil

2 large onions, chopped

2 large garlic cloves, crushed

2 tsp crushed dried chillies

2 thin red chillies, deseeded, if liked, and chopped

1 tsp grated fresh root ginger

1 tsp ground turmeric

¼ tsp ground cloves

2 tsp ground cumin

1 tsp ground coriander

1 tbsp garam masala

400g lean diced pork

225g pig's liver, trimmed and diced

1 tsp salt

250ml water

3 tbsp balsamic vinegar

1 bay leaf

2 large potatoes, cut into large chunks

2 carrots, cut into thick slices

6 tbsp ground almonds

2 tbsp chopped fresh coriander

1 lemon, cut into wedges

To serve

Basmati rice

1. Heat the oil in the pressure cooker. Add the onions and garlic and fry, stirring, for 2 minutes. Add all the spices and stir for 30 seconds. Add the pork and liver and fry, stirring, for 2–3 minutes until browned all over. Stir in the salt, water, vinegar and bay leaf.

2. Bring to the boil, stirring and scraping up any sediment from the bottom of the pressure cooker. Add the potatoes, carrots and almonds.

3. Cover with the lid and bring up to High pressure, then reduce the heat and cook for 20 minutes.

4. Remove from the heat and reduce the pressure quickly under cold water.

5. Garnish with chopped fresh coriander and wedges of lemon and serve with basmati rice.

This is a delicious cook-in-advance loaf that's great with new potatoes and salad or in thinner slices in torpedo rolls with pickles and mustard. It's great for picnics too!

Serves 4 | Preparation time: 10 minutes | Cooking time: 35 minutes

Pork Meatloaf to Eat Cold

150g bacon pieces

225g minced pork

115g good-quality pork sausagemeat

75g fresh white breadcrumbs

1 small onion, grated

1 tbsp chopped fresh sage

1 tsp tomato purée

Salt and freshly ground black pepper

500ml boiling water

1 tbsp lemon juice

1. Grease a 450g loaf tin and line with baking parchment. Pick over the bacon pieces, discarding any rind, bones or gristle. Mince or finely chop in a food processor. Tip into a large bowl and add all the remaining ingredients, except the water and lemon juice, seasoning well with salt and pepper. Mix with your hands until thoroughly combined. Pack into the loaf tin and cover with baking parchment then foil, twisting and folding under the rim to secure. Place the water and lemon juice in the pressure cooker and add the trivet and the steaming basket. Place the loaf tin in the basket.

2. Cover with the lid and bring up to High pressure, then cook for 35 minutes.

3. Remove from the heat and allow the pressure to reduce slowly at room temperature.

4. Remove the loaf tin from the pan and weigh down with heavy weights or a can of food. Leave to cool, then chill until firm.

5. Turn out and serve cold, cut into slices.

This is easy-to-make peasant food from the Alsace region of France. It means you eat rather a lot of meat for one meal but at least you get a lot of cabbage too! It is so delicious cooked in a pressure cooker because it is tender and full of flavour in no time.

Serves 4 | Preparation time: 8 minutes | Cooking time: 20 minutes

Choucroûte Garni

A large knob of butter

4 chicken thighs

1 onion, thinly sliced

1 large garlic clove, crushed

6 juniper berries, crushed

½ tsp ground coriander

A large pinch of ground cloves

150ml fruity white wine

150ml chicken stock

Salt and freshly ground black pepper

450g piece of speck or other smoked
streaky pork

4 large frankfurters

810g jar of sauerkraut

900g potatoes, peeled and cut into
bite-sized pieces

1 bay leaf

To serve

Mustard

1. Heat the butter in the pressure cooker and brown the chicken thighs quickly on all sides. Remove from the pan. Add the onion and garlic, fry gently, stirring, for 2 minutes to soften. Stir in the spices, wine and stock and bring to the boil. Season well with salt and pepper.

2. Wash the sauerkraut well and stir into the pan. Add all the meats, (including the browned chicken) and the bay leaf.

3. Cover with the lid and bring up to High pressure, then reduce the heat and cook for 12 minutes.

4. Remove from the heat and reduce the pressure quickly under cold water.

5. Put the potatoes in the steaming basket and place it on top of the meats. Sprinkle with a little salt.

6. Cover with the lid, bring back to pressure and cook for 5 minutes.

7. Remove from the heat and reduce the pressure quickly under cold water.

8. Lift out the potatoes and keep them warm. Then remove the pieces of pork and the frankfurters. Cut the smoked pork into chunks. Spoon the sauerkraut onto plates with a slotted spoon. Top with the pieces of pork, chicken and the frankfurters. Serve hot with the potatoes and mustard.

This recipe has lots of delicious sauce and makes a pleasant change from a stir-fry. Serve over plain rice and add a crisp green salad to accompany. For maximum convenience, I like to cook the rice in a separate pan while the pork is cooking.

Serves 4 | Preparation time: 20 minutes | Cooking time: 12 minutes

Braised Sweet and Sour Pork with Fresh Pineapple

1 small fresh pineapple

2 tbsp sunflower oil

500g boneless belly pork slices, rinded and cut into bite-sized chunks

120ml orange juice

100ml chicken stock

3 tbsp soy sauce

2 garlic cloves, crushed

1 tbsp tomato purée

1 tbsp soft light brown sugar

½ tsp Chinese five-spice powder

2 large carrots, peeled and cut into matchsticks

2 celery sticks, cut into matchsticks

1 bunch of spring onions, trimmed and cut into short diagonal lengths

100g mangetout

100g fresh beansprouts

2–3 tbsp cornflour

2–3 tbsp water

To serve

Plain boiled rice

1. Cut the top and bottom off the pineapple. Hold it upright on a board and cut off the skin in downward slices all round. Cut the flesh into thick slices, then cut into cubes, discarding any hard central core. Set aside.

2. Heat the oil in the pressure cooker, add the pork and fry until browned on all sides. Add the orange juice, stock, soy sauce, garlic, tomato purée, spice and sugar.

3. Cover with the lid and bring up to High pressure, then reduce the heat and cook for 10 minutes.

4. Remove from the heat and reduce the pressure quickly under cold water.

5. Add the pineapple and vegetables, re-cover with the lid and bring up to High pressure, then reduce the pressure immediately under cold water (so the vegetables retain some crispy texture).

6. Blend the cornflour with the water and stir into the open cooker. Bring to the boil and cook for 1 minute, stirring. Taste and add more soy sauce or a little more sugar, to taste.

7. Serve spooned over plain rice in bowls.

The combination of ham and butter beans is one of my favourites. Choose a cheaper collar bacon joint to dice for this recipe as there's no point in buying more expensive gammon. Use two cans of butter beans, if you prefer, instead of dried. If you do so, make up the liquid to 500ml with water and begin at step 4.

Serves 4 | Preparation time: 15 minutes, plus soaking | Cooking time: 40 minutes

Ham and Butter Bean Stew

225g dried butter beans, soaked in cold water for several hours or boiling water for 1 hour

700g bacon joint, skin and fat removed, then cut into cubes

2 leeks, cut into chunks

2 large carrots, peeled and thickly sliced

1 turnip, diced

1 tbsp chicken stock concentrate

1 bay leaf

3 tbsp dried milk powder

2 tbsp plain flour

6 tbsp water

2 tbsp chopped fresh parsley

Salt and freshly ground black pepper

To serve

Crusty bread

1. Drain the soaked beans. Put them in the pressure cooker and just cover with cold water so the cooker is not more than one-third full. Bring to the boil in the open cooker, skim any scum that rises to the surface using a slotted spoon.

2. Cover with the lid and bring up to High pressure over a medium heat, then cook for 20 minutes.

3. Remove from the heat and reduce the pressure quickly under cold water.

4. Drain the beans, reserving the liquid, then return them to the cooker. Add the bacon, vegetables and 500ml of the reserved cooking water. Add the chicken stock concentrate and bay leaf.

5. Cover with the lid and bring up to High pressure, then reduce the heat and cook for 20 minutes.

6. Remove from the heat and reduce the pressure quickly under cold water.

7. Discard the bay leaf. Blend the milk powder, flour and water to a smooth paste and stir into the pot. Bring to the boil and cook for 2 minutes, stirring. Add the parsley and season to taste. Serve hot in bowls with slices of crusty bread.

If you serve this hot, there will be some left to have cold too. This simple, traditional complete meal can be served with parsley sauce, if you prefer, but I love the sweet taste of the onions with it.

Serves 6 | Preparation time: 15 minutes | Cooking time: 18 minutes

Boiled Ham with Onion Sauce

1kg joint bacon or gammon, soaked if necessary, according to packet instructions

1 bay leaf

12 black peppercorns

3 large carrots, peeled and cut into thick chunks

4 large potatoes, peeled and quartered

2 leeks, cut into thick chunks

100g frozen peas, thawed

For the sauce

2 onions, quartered and thickly sliced

A large knob of butter

300ml milk

3 tbsp plain flour

Salt and freshly ground black pepper

1. Put the gammon in the pressure cooker and just cover with cold water. Bring to the boil in the open cooker, then skim off any scum that rises to the surface. Add the bay leaf and peppercorns.

2. Cover with the lid and bring up to High pressure, then reduce the heat and cook for 13 minutes.

3. Remove from the heat and reduce the pressure quickly under cold water. Add the carrots, potatoes and leeks. Cover, bring back to High pressure, reduce the heat and cook for 5 minutes.

4. Carefully lift out the vegetables and keep warm. Transfer the ham to a carving dish and keep warm.

5. Put the peas in the steaming basket on the trivet in the cooker.

6. Cover with the lid, bring up to pressure, then reduce the pressure immediately under cold water.

7. Meanwhile, put the onions and butter a small saucepan. Cook, stirring, for 2 minutes until softening but not browning. Add all but about 4 tbsp of the milk, bring to the boil, reduce the heat, cover and simmer for about 5 minutes or until the onions are soft. Blend the flour with the remaining milk and stir into the sauce. Cook, stirring, for 2 minutes until thickened. Season to taste.

8. Carve the ham and serve with the potatoes, carrots, leeks, peas, some of the broth strained into a sauce boat and the onion sauce.

There will be some cold you can slice for sandwiches after you've enjoyed this fabulous, succulent ham hot. Use the strained stock as a basis for a split pea or lentil soup, too.

Serves 6 | Preparation time: 5 minutes (plus soaking, if necessary) | Cooking time: 45 minutes

Honey Roast Ham

1kg joint bacon or gammon, soaked, if necessary, according to instructions

1 bay leaf

1 small onion, quartered

12 black peppercorns

2 tbsp thick honey

1 tbsp grainy mustard

200ml cider

To serve

Mustard, jacket-baked potatoes, broccoli and baby corn

1. Put the gammon in the pressure cooker. Just cover with cold water. Bring to the boil in the open cooker and skim the surface. Add the bay leaf, onion and peppercorns.

2. Cover with the lid and bring up to High pressure, then reduce the heat and cook for 10 minutes.

3. Remove from the heat and reduce the pressure quickly under cold water.

4. Carefully lift out of the cooker and place in a roasting tin. Remove the rind and score the fat in a criss-cross pattern.

5. Preheat the oven to 190°C/gas 5.

6. Blend the honey and mustard together and spread all over the fat. Pour the cider around the pork but don't pour it over the glaze. Roast in the oven for 30 minutes until a rich brown.

7. Transfer the meat to a carving dish. Put the roasting tin on the hob and boil the juices, scraping up any sediment, until reduced and thickened slightly. Taste and re-season, if necessary.

8. Serve the gammon carved in thick slices with the cider juices spooned over. Serve mustard on the side, with jacket potatoes, broccoli and baby corn as accompaniments.

Chapter 11

Chicken

You will be rewarded with better flavour if you buy a free-range chicken rather than a cheap one that may be pumped full of water; ethically it is sound judgement too. For most recipes I recommend removing the skin from joints before cooking but sometimes it is necessary to retain it for the flavour and colour it gives to the finished dish. You will always be told when to do this. It is sometimes cheaper to buy a small whole chicken and cut it into quarters yourself rather than buying ready-prepared portions – particularly when chickens are on special offer. You do need a heavy sharp knife or poultry shears to do this, though.

Although this is a complete meal, I find a crisp green salad rounds if off as it offsets the richness of the casserole. I love bulgur as a change from couscous but this can be used instead if preferred.

Serves 4 | Preparation time: 15 minutes | Cooking time: 14 minutes

Chicken Tagine with Prunes and Bulgur

4 chicken leg portions

1 preserved lemon, quartered

A knob of butter

2 onions, thinly sliced

1 green pepper, thinly sliced

900ml boiling chicken stock

225g baby chantenay carrots, peeled and topped and tailed

100g baby corn cobs, cut into short lengths

1 tsp ground cinnamon

½ tsp dried oregano

100g ready-to-eat stoned prunes, halved

2 tbsp clear honey

2 tbsp tomato purée

Salt and freshly ground black pepper

2 tbsp sesame seeds, toasted

225g bulgur

1. Rub the chicken all over with the lemon. Heat the butter in the pressure cooker, add the chicken and brown it quickly. Remove from the cooker. Add the onions and pepper to the cooker and fry for 2 minutes, stirring. Return the chicken to the pan with the lemon quarters, 300ml of the stock and all the remaining ingredients except the sesame seeds and bulgur.

2. Meanwhile, put the bulgur in a heatproof bowl. Stir in the remaining stock, then cover with foil, twisting and folding under the rim to secure it. Place the bowl in the cooker with the chicken.

3. Cover with the lid and bring up to High pressure, then reduce the heat and cook for 10 minutes.

4. Remove from the heat and reduce the pressure quickly under cold water.

5. Remove the bulgur and fluff up with a fork. Taste and re-season the tagine as necessary. Spoon the bulgur onto plates, top with the tagine and serve sprinkled with the sesame seeds.

This is a recipe where the pressure cooker works for you alongside another old favourite – the frying pan! It means the two elements of the dish can be cooked at the same time, which makes for an even quicker meal.

Serves 4 | Preparation time: 15 minutes | Cooking time: 15 minutes

Chicken with Cream and Grapes on Rosti

4 corn-fed chicken breasts with skin

A knob of unsalted butter

5 tbsp sunflower oil

1 onion, finely chopped

300ml dry white wine

A large pinch of caster sugar

1 tbsp chopped fresh tarragon

Salt and freshly ground black pepper

2 tbsp plain flour

4 tbsp water

150ml single cream

100g seedless white grapes, halved

For the rosti

2 large potatoes

1 small onion

1 egg

To garnish

A few sprigs of tarragon

To serve

A green salad

1. Wipe the chicken with kitchen paper. Heat the butter and 1 tbsp of the oil in the pressure cooker, add the chicken and fry to brown on all sides. Remove from the cooker with a slotted spoon. Add the onion and cook gently for 3 minutes until a pale golden brown. Return the chicken to the pan and add the wine, sugar, tarragon and some salt and pepper.

2. Cover with the lid and bring up to High pressure, then reduce the heat and cook for 10 minutes.

3. Remove from the heat and reduce the pressure quickly under cold water.

4. Lift the chicken out of the cooker and keep it warm. Blend the flour with the water, then stir it into the cooking liquid. Bring to the boil, then cook for 2 minutes, stirring. Add the cream and grapes, and re-season if necessary.

5. Meanwhile, grate the potatoes, put them into a colander and squeeze out as much moisture as possible. Grate the onion and add it to the potatoes. Add plenty of salt and pepper and mix together, then mix in the beaten egg to bind.

6. Heat the remaining oil in a large frying pan. Divide the rosti mixture into four equal portions. Shape into rough cakes and fry in the oil for about 3 minutes on each side until crisp and golden. Drain on kitchen paper.

7. Place the rosti on warm plates and put the chicken on top. Spoon the sauce over and garnish with sprigs of tarragon.

A delicious dish that's elegant enough for a special occasion or simple enough for a midweek meal. The perfect all-purpose recipe! I like to serve it with mangetout, cooked very quickly in the microwave or boiled briefly in lightly salted water.

Serves 4 | Preparation time: 15 minutes | Cooking time: 10 minutes

Casseroled Chicken Wrapped in Bacon

4 rindless rashers of streaky bacon

4 skinless chicken breasts

1 tbsp sunflower oil

A large knob of butter

1 onion, chopped

1 garlic clove, crushed

100g chestnut mushrooms, sliced

150ml dry white wine

150ml chicken stock

½ tsp dried thyme

Salt and freshly ground black pepper

500g potatoes, peeled and cut into bite-sized chunks

3–4 tbsp plain flour

3–4 tbsp water

2 tsp soy sauce

To garnish

2 tbsp chopped fresh parsley

1. Stretch the bacon rashers with the back of a knife. Wrap one rasher round each chicken breast and secure with cocktail sticks.

2. Heat the oil and butter in the pressure cooker, add the chicken and fry to brown it all over. Remove with a slotted spoon. Add the onion, garlic and mushrooms to the pan and fry, stirring, for 2 minutes. Stir in the wine, stock, thyme and some seasoning and return the chicken to the pan.

3. Cover with the lid and bring up to High pressure, then reduce the heat and cook for 2 minutes.

4. Remove from the heat and reduce the pressure quickly under cold water.

5. Put the potatoes in the steamer basket and lay them on top of the chicken. Season lightly with salt.

6. Cover with the lid and bring up to High pressure, then cook a further 4 minutes.

7. Remove from the heat and reduce the pressure quickly under cold water.

8. Lift out the potatoes and keep warm, then carefully lift the chicken out of the cooker, pull out the sticks and keep the chicken warm, too.

9. Blend 3 tbsp flour with 3 tbsp water and stir into the pan. Bring to the boil, stirring until thickened. If the sauce has not thickened as much as you like, blend the further tbsp flour and water together and stir into the pan. Boil the thickened sauce for 2 minutes, stirring. Stir in the soy sauce to colour it slightly, then taste and re-season, if necessary.

10. Put the potatoes on serving plates and sprinkle with chopped parsley. Put the chicken alongside and spoon the sauce over. Serve hot.

A classic dish that couldn't be left out as it is so easy to cook in the pressure cooker. It's good with jacket baked potatoes but, rather than put the oven on, prick them all over and microwave for 3–4 minutes each until tender, then brown under a preheated grill to crisp the skin.

Serves 4 | Preparation time: 15 minutes | Cooking time: 12 minutes

Coq au Vin

4 chicken leg portions

3 tbsp olive oil

A knob of butter

12 button onions

100g bacon lardons

100g button mushrooms

150ml red wine

150ml chicken stock

1 tbsp brandy

1 bouquet garni

Salt and freshly ground black pepper

3 tbsp plain flour

3 tbsp water

To garnish

2 slices of white bread, crusts removed

Sprigs of watercress

To serve

French bread and a crisp green salad

1. Wipe the chicken with kitchen paper. Heat 1 tbsp of the oil with the butter in the pressure cooker. Add the chicken portions and fry to brown on all sides, then remove from the pan. Add the onions and bacon and brown them quickly, stirring. Remove from the pan and set aside.

2. Return the chicken to the pan. Add the mushrooms, wine, stock, brandy and bouquet garni. Season with salt and pepper.

3. Cover with the lid, bring up to High pressure, then reduce the heat and cook for 6 minutes.

4. Remove from the heat and reduce the pressure quickly under cold water.

5. Add the onions and bacon, cover with the lid and bring up to High pressure again and cook for 4 minutes.

6. Remove from the heat and reduce the pressure quickly under cold water.

7. Carefully lift the chicken, onions, bacon and mushrooms out of the pan and keep them warm. Discard the bouquet garni. Blend the flour with the water and stir into the cooking liquid. Bring to the boil and boil for 2 minutes, stirring all the time until thickened. Taste and re-season, if necessary. Return the chicken, bacon and vegetables to the pan.

8. Meanwhile, cut each bread slice into four triangles. Fry the bread in a frying pan in the remaining oil until golden brown on both sides. Drain on kitchen paper.

9. Serve the chicken, garnished with the toast triangles and watercress with French bread and a crisp green salad.

You could just add baby potatoes to the vegetable mix cooked with the chicken but I prefer to sauté some diced potatoes (and sprinkle with a little chopped garlic) whilst the chicken is cooking to serve alongside for a bit of different flavour, colour and texture.

Serves 4 | Preparation time: 15 minutes | Cooking time: 7 minutes

Braised Stuffed Chicken Rolls with Roots and Broad Beans

40g fresh white breadcrumbs

2 tbsp chopped fresh parsley

1 tbsp chopped fresh rosemary

1 tbsp chopped fresh thyme

Salt and freshly ground black pepper

1 egg, beaten

4 skinless chicken breasts

2 large carrots, cut in thick slices

½ celeriac, cut into small chunks

½ small swede, cut into small chunks

150g fresh shelled or frozen broad beans

12 small waxy potatoes, scrubbed

450ml chicken stock

1 bay leaf

3 tbsp cornflour

5 tbsp single cream

To garnish

1 tbsp chopped parsley

1. Mix the breadcrumbs with the herbs and some salt and pepper. Stir in the beaten egg to bind. Put the chicken breasts one at a time in a plastic bag and beat with a rolling pin or meat mallet to flatten. Spread the stuffing over the surfaces, roll up and secure with cocktail sticks. Put the prepared vegetables in the pressure cooker and place the chicken on top. Add the stock and bay leaf.

2. Cover with the lid and bring up to High pressure, then reduce the heat and cook for 6 minutes.

3. Remove from the heat and reduce the pressure quickly under cold water.

4. Carefully lift out the rolls and the vegetables and keep them warm. Blend the cornflour with the cream and stir into the stock. Bring to the boil and simmer for 1 minute, stirring. Taste and add more seasoning if necessary.

5. Put the chicken and root vegetables on plates. Spoon the sauce over. Garnish with chopped parsley and serve hot.

Like the sweet and sour recipe, this gives delicious saucy-type Chinese without all that stir-frying! Serve it on a bed of Chinese noodles, which can be reconstituted in minutes when the chicken is nearly ready, although you could cook rice, if you prefer.

Serves 4 | Preparation time: 10 minutes | Cooking time: 8 minutes

Braised Chicken in Black Bean Sauce

500g diced chicken breast

150ml chicken stock

4 tbsp black bean sauce

1 large garlic clove, crushed

2 tsp grated fresh root ginger

½ tsp Chinese five-spice powder

4 tbsp soy sauce

2 tbsp mirin or dry sherry

1 tbsp clear honey

2 red peppers, cut into thin strips

100g oyster mushrooms, cut into thick slices

2 tbsp cornflour

2 tbsp water

5cm piece of cucumber, cut into matchsticks

To serve

Chinese egg noodles

Sweet chilli sauce

1. Put the chicken in the pressure cooker with the stock, black bean sauce, garlic, ginger, five-spice powder, soy sauce, mirin and honey.

2. Cover with the lid and bring up to High pressure, then reduce the heat and cook for 5 minutes.

3. Remove from the heat and reduce the pressure quickly under cold water.

4. Add the peppers and mushrooms. Bring up to pressure again and cook for 1 minute.

5. Remove from the heat and reduce the pressure quickly under cold water.

6. Blend the cornflour with the water and stir into the cooker. Cook, stirring, for 2 minutes until thickened and clear.

7. Spoon onto the Chinese egg noodles in warm bowls. Sprinkle with the cucumber and drizzle with a little sweet chilli sauce before serving.

This is a family favourite for a quick mid-week meal. I cook broccoli separately to serve with it but you could have peas or just serve with a green salad. The sauce can also be thickened with a little cornflour blended with water at the end if preferred.

Serves 4 | Preparation time: 5 minutes | Cooking time: 12 minutes

Chicken and Tomato Casserole

1 large onion, finely chopped

2 carrots, peeled and finely chopped

A large knob of butter

4 skinless chicken breasts

100g cup mushrooms, quartered

400g can of chopped tomatoes

150ml chicken stock

3 tbsp medium-dry sherry

2 tbsp tomato purée

½ tsp dried mixed herbs

Salt and freshly ground black pepper

400g baby potatoes, scrubbed

To serve

Broccoli

1. Brown the onion and carrots in the butter in the pressure cooker, stirring, for 2 minutes. Add the chicken breasts and cook briefly on each side. Add the mushrooms, the can of tomatoes and the stock. Blend the sherry with the tomato purée and stir in. Add the herbs and season with salt and pepper.

2. Cover with the lid, bring up to High pressure, then reduce the heat and cook for 6 minutes.

3. Remove from the heat and reduce the pressure quickly under cold water. Spoon off any fat. Put the potatoes in the steamer basket and add to the pan. Sprinkle with a little salt.

4. Cover with the lid, bring back to pressure and cook for 4 minutes.

5. Remove from the heat and reduce the pressure quickly under cold water.

6. Lift the potatoes out of the pan and keep warm. Taste and re-season the chicken if necessary. Serve the casserole with the potatoes and broccoli.

All the flavours of the Deep South, cooked together in one pot. It makes a delicious meal in winter and summer, funnily enough! The gumbo is usually served with the rice on top but spoon it over rice, in the more usual fashion if preferred.

Serves 6 | Preparation time: 10 minutes | Cooking time: 15 minutes

Chicken Gumbo

40g butter

1 tbsp sunflower oil

2 boneless belly pork slices, rinded and cut into chunks

350g diced chicken breast

2 onions, chopped

2 celery sticks, chopped

2 garlic cloves, crushed

250g okra, trimmed and cut into thirds

100g baby corn, cut into chunks

400g can of chopped tomatoes

250ml chicken stock

225g raw, shelled king prawns

75g frozen peas

Tabasco sauce

Salt and freshly ground black pepper

To serve

Plain boiled rice

1. Melt half the butter with the oil in the pressure cooker. Brown the pork until the fat runs. Stir in the chicken, onions, celery and garlic and fry for 2 minutes. Add the okra and fry for 2 minutes, stirring. Stir in the corn, tomatoes and stock.

2. Cover with the lid and bring up to High pressure, then reduce the heat and cook for 5 minutes.

3. Remove from the heat and reduce the pressure quickly under cold water.

4. Add the prawns and peas, cover with the lid, bring back to pressure, then reduce the pressure immediately under cold water.

5. Season with Tabasco, salt and pepper to taste. Serve the gumbo in bowls with a large spoonful of plain boiled rice on top.

Another easy, all-in-one meal. The chicken literally falls off the bones it is so tender and the stuffing gives loads of added flavour. It's important that the chicken isn't too big to fit in the cooker comfortably so don't be tempted to buy a bigger one!

Serves 4 | Preparation time: 15 minutes | Cooking time: 30 minutes

Stuffed Pot Roast Chicken with Vegetables

1.2kg oven-ready chicken

4 tbsp fresh breadcrumbs

100g smooth liver pâté with garlic

2 tbsp chopped fresh parsley

1 tbsp chopped fresh thyme

40g butter

2 carrots, peeled and cut into thick chunks

2 leeks, cut into thick chunks

150g green beans, trimmed and cut into thirds

400g baby potatoes, scrubbed

Salt and freshly ground black pepper

1 bay leaf

300ml chicken stock

2 tbsp cornflour

2 tbsp water

Soy sauce (optional)

1. Wipe the chicken inside and out with kitchen paper and pull off any fat just inside the body cavity.

2. Mash the breadcrumbs with the pâté, parsley and thyme. Use to stuff the neck end of the bird and secure with cocktail sticks.

3. Melt the butter in the pressure cooker and brown the chicken all over. Remove from the pan. Add the carrots, leeks, beans and potatoes and cook, stirring, for 2 minutes. Put the chicken on top. Season well and add the bay leaf. Add the stock. Cover, bring up to High pressure, then reduce the heat and cook for 25 minutes.

4. Remove from the heat and reduce the pressure quickly under cold water. Check the chicken is cooked – the juices should run clear when pierced at the thickest part of the thigh.

5. Carefully lift out the chicken and put on a carving dish. Discard the bay leaf. Lift out the vegetables with a draining spoon and keep them warm. Spoon off any excess fat from the cooking juices. Blend the cornflour with the water and stir in. Bring to the boil and cook for 1 minute, stirring. Taste and re-season, if necessary. Add a splash of soy sauce, if liked.

6. Carve (or you may just have to cut it up as it will be very tender) the chicken and the stuffing and serve with the vegetables and gravy.

This is one of my favourite curries and is cooked very quickly in the pressure cooker. Put a pan of water for rice on before you start cooking the curry. The glorious pink raita is a lovely change from the more usual cucumber and mint one.

Serves 4 | Preparation time:15 minutes | Cooking time: 10 minutes

Chicken Bhuna Masala with Beetroot Raita

1 tbsp sunflower oil

A large knob of butter

4 skinless chicken breasts, cut into thick pieces or 8 skinless chicken thighs

2 green chillies, deseeded and chopped

2 large onions, finely chopped

1 tsp grated fresh root ginger

2 tsp ground cumin

4 cardamom pods, split and seeds extracted

1/2 tsp ground turmeric

1/4 tsp ground cloves

1 large garlic clove, crushed

400g can of chopped tomatoes

150ml chicken stock

Salt and freshly ground black pepper

2 tbsp chopped fresh coriander

For the raita

1 tbsp cumin seeds

2 cooked beetroot, grated

120ml thick, plain yoghurt

1 tbsp chopped fresh mint

To serve

Basmati rice and a side salad

1. Heat the oil and butter in the pressure cooker. Add the chicken and onions and brown quickly, stirring, for 3 minutes.

2. Add the remaining ingredients except the coriander.

3. Cover with the lid and bring up to High pressure, then reduce the heat and cook for 5 minutes.

4. Reduce the pressure quickly. Boil rapidly in the open cooker for a few minutes to reduce and thicken the sauce. Stir in the coriander.

5. Meanwhile, toast the cumin seeds in a dry frying pan for about 30 seconds until fragrant. Tip into a bowl and add the grated beetroot, yoghurt and mint. Season lightly with salt and pepper.

6. Serve the bhuna masala on rice with the beetroot raita and a side salad.

If you can't be bothered to cook some ribbon noodles from scratch, buy some ready-to-wok ones and just pop them in boiling water for a minute or so. I always keep various sizes of these noodles in the cupboard for speedy suppers.

Serves 4 | Preparation time: 10 minutes | Cooking time: 10 minutes

Lemon Chicken Bites with Pesto Sauce

1 tbsp water

1 tbsp cornflour

3 tbsp pesto sauce

3 tbsp dry cider, white wine or vermouth

Salt and freshly ground black pepper

8 skinless chicken thighs

1 lemon, halved and sliced

1 tbsp lemon juice

225g tagliatelle

To garnish

Fresh sprigs of basil

To serve

A mixed salad

1. Mix the water and cornflour together in a shallow dish that will fit in the pressure cooker. Stir in the pesto, cider or wine and a little salt and pepper. Add the chicken thighs and mix to coat completely. If time, leave to marinate in the fridge for an hour or two.

2. Tuck half the lemon slices in between the chicken, reserving the remainder for garnish. Cover tightly with foil, twisting and folding under the rim to secure.

3. Place the dish in the steaming basket of the pressure cooker. Put 500ml water in the cooker with the lemon juice. Stand the basket on the trivet in the cooker. Cover with the lid, bring up to High pressure, then reduce the heat and cook for 10 minutes.

4. Remove from the heat and reduce the pressure quickly under cold water.

5. Meanwhile, cook the tagliatelle according to packet directions. Drain.

6. Lift the chicken out of the cooker. Pile the noodles on plates. Discard the cooked lemon slices. Lift the chicken out of the sauce and place on the noodles. Stir the sauce well and spoon over. Garnish with sprigs of basil and the reserved lemon slices. Serve with a mixed salad.

The chicken is marinated in the spices, garlic and onion before cooking in a rich tomato sauce. If time is short, you can omit the marinating but the flavour won't be as good.

Serves 4 | Preparation time: 5 minutes, plus marinating | Cooking time: 10 minutes

Sautéed Chicken in Tomato Curry Sauce

2 large onions, finely chopped

1 large garlic clove, crushed

2 fat green chillies, deseeded and finely chopped

1 tsp grated fresh root ginger (or ginger purée)

$\frac{1}{2}$ tsp ground turmeric

$\frac{1}{2}$ tsp salt

4 skinless chicken breasts, cubed

2 tbsp sunflower oil

A knob of butter

400g can of chopped tomatoes

2 tbsp tomato purée

150ml chicken stock

1 tsp caster sugar

Freshly ground black pepper

3 tbsp chopped fresh coriander

4 tbsp plain yogurt

To serve

Plain basmati rice

Mango chutney

1. Mix the onion and garlic with all the spices and the salt. Add the chicken, mix well and leave to marinate for at least 2 hours or preferably all day or overnight.

2. Heat the oil and butter in the pressure cooker. Add the chicken and brown quickly all over. Add the tomatoes, tomatoe purée, stock, sugar, a good grinding of pepper and 1 tbsp of the coriander.

3. Cover with the lid, bring up to High pressure, then reduce the heat and cook for 4 minutes.

4. Reduce the pressure quickly under cold water.

5. Remove the lid and boil rapidly for a few minutes until the liquid is reduced and the chicken is bathed in a rich sauce.

6. Taste and re-season, if necessary. Spoon the curry over rice, add a dollop of plain yogurt and sprinkle with the remaining chopped coriander. Serve topped with a dollop of mango chutney.

Chapter 12

Other Poultry and Game

Here you will also find recipes using duck and turkey, game birds and venison. Guinea fowl are actually farmed birds so not technically game. But they make a delicious alternative to chicken and can be cooked in the same way. Game birds, in particular, can sometimes be tough and dry but in the pressure cooker they become tender and juicy. As with the other meat recipes, sometimes you'll have recipes for complete meals cooked in the pressure cooker, sometimes it will be used just for an integral part of the finished dish. In all cases you will have delicious dishes cooked quickly and efficiently using the minimum of fuel and giving you maximum flavour!

This moist and tasty pilaf needs careful timing. Leave it too long and it will be too soft. If you've not cooked rice in the pressure cooker before, try cooking with plain rice as an accompaniment first so you get use to the technique.

Serves 4 | Preparation time: 15 minutes | Cooking time: 15 minutes

Turkey and Vegetable Pilaf

2 tbsp olive oil

1 onion, chopped

1 garlic clove, crushed

225g diced turkey meat

1 red pepper, diced

1 large courgette, diced

225g long-grain rice

2 tbsp tomato purée

450ml chicken stock

A large pinch of ground cloves

1 tsp ground cinnamon

50g stoned black olives

4 pieces of semi-dried tomato, chopped

Salt and freshly ground black pepper

100g feta cheese, cubed

To garnish

Torn fresh mint leaves

To serve

Flat breads

Mixed salad

1. Heat the oil in the pressure cooker. Add the onion, garlic and turkey and fry for 2 minutes, stirring. Stir in the pepper, courgette and rice until glistening. Blend the tomato purée with the stock and stir into the pan with cloves, cinnamon, olives, semi-dried tomatoes and a little salt and pepper. Bring to the boil in the open cooker, stirring.

2. Cover with the lid and bring up to High pressure over a medium heat, then reduce the heat to low and cook for 5 minutes.

3. Remove from the heat and allow the pressure to reduce slowly at room temperature.

4. Stir in the feta, re-cover and leave for 5 minutes. Taste and re-season, if necessary. Spoon into warm bowls and sprinkle with torn mint. Serve with flat breads and a mixed salad.

A tasty curry that can be made with chicken instead. If you prefer a beef or lamb one, prepare the same way but cook for 15 minutes at High pressure. The rice is added for the last five minutes so you have a complete meal (though I like to serve a side salad as well).

Serves 4 | Preparation time: 15 minutes | Cooking time: 10 minutes

Simple Turkey Curry

2 tbsp sunflower oil

2 onions, chopped

500g diced turkey meat

1 green pepper, diced

100g button mushrooms, halved

1 tbsp Madras curry paste

300ml chicken stock

2 tbsp mango chutney

50g frozen peas

2 tomatoes, skinned and chopped

225g long-grain rice

450ml boiling water

Salt and freshly ground black pepper

50g creamed coconut

2 tbsp chopped fresh coriander

To serve

Poppadoms

1. Heat the oil in the pressure cooker and fry the onions, stirring, for 2 minutes, then stir in the turkey, pepper, mushrooms and curry paste and fry for 30 seconds. Stir in the stock, chutney, peas and tomatoes.

2. Cover with the lid and bring up to High pressure, then reduce the heat and cook for 2 minutes.

3. Remove from the heat and reduce the pressure quickly under cold water.

4. Put the rice and boiling water into a bowl large enough to allow the rice to swell. Add a large pinch of salt. Cover with foil, twisting and folding under the rim to secure. Push the curry pieces to one side so you can place the bowl in the cooker. Re-cover with the lid, bring back to High pressure and cook for 5 minutes.

5. Remove from the heat and allow the pressure to reduce slowly at room temperature.

6. Lift out the bowl of rice. Stir the coconut into the curry, stirring over a gentle heat until dissolved and the sauce thickens. Stir in the coriander, taste and season as necessary. Fluff up the rice with a fork and serve with the curry and poppadoms.

Redcurrant jelly, like cranberries, goes really well with turkey. When fresh currants are in season, throw a few into the sauce and simmer a minute or two before serving and garnish with small bunches of them too.

Serves 4 | Preparation time: 10 minutes | Cooking time: 15 minutes

Braised Turkey with Redcurrant and Mushrooms

2 tbsp sunflower oil

4 turkey breast steaks

2 onions, sliced

2 carrots, peeled and thinly sliced

100g chestnut mushrooms, sliced

450ml chicken stock

1 tsp dried mixed herbs

Salt and freshly ground black pepper

400g baby potatoes, scrubbed

2 tbsp redcurrant jelly

2 tbsp plain flour

1 tbsp soy sauce

1 tbsp water

1 tbsp chopped, fresh parsley

To serve

Baby Brussels sprouts

1. Heat the oil in the pressure cooker and quickly brown the turkey steaks. Remove from the pan with a slotted spoon. Add the onions and carrots and fry quickly for 2 minutes, stirring. Add the mushrooms and fry for a further 1 minute. Lay the turkey on top of the vegetables and pour over the stock. Add the herbs and season with salt and pepper.

2. Cover with the lid and bring up to High pressure, then reduce the heat and cook for 6 minutes.

3. Remove from the heat and reduce the pressure quickly under cold water.

4. Put the potatoes in the steamer basket and season lightly with salt. Put in the pressure cooker, re-cover with the lid, bring back to High pressure, reduce the heat and cook for 4 minutes.

5. Remove from the heat and reduce the pressure quickly under cold water.

6. Lift out the potatoes and keep them warm. Carefully lift the turkey out of the cooker, transfer to warm serving plates and keep it warm.

7. Stir the redcurrant jelly into the cooking liquid. Blend the flour with the soy sauce and water and stir in. Bring to the boil and cook for 2 minutes, stirring all the time. Taste and re-season, if necessary.

8. Spoon the sauce over the turkey and sprinkle with chopped parsley. Serve with the new potatoes and Brussels sprouts.

This is equally delicious made with lamb or beef instead of turkey. Simply trim the meat to remove any fat or gristle and cook in the same way, although for beef, cook for 16 minutes before adding the potatoes, and for lamb or pork cook for 11 minutes.

Serves 4 | Preparation time: 15 minutes | Cooking time: 17 minutes

Turkey Goulash

700g diced turkey

3 tbsp plain flour

Salt and freshly ground black pepper

2 tbsp sunflower oil

2 onions, chopped

1 garlic clove, crushed

1 green pepper, diced

2 carrots, peeled and cut into thick slices

150ml chicken stock

150ml passata

1 tbsp sweet paprika

½ tsp caster sugar

4 large potatoes, peeled and cut into chunks

To garnish

Soured cream or crème fraîche

A little chopped fresh parsley

1. Toss the turkey in the flour, seasoned with a little salt and pepper. Heat the oil in the pressure cooker and fry the onions, stirring, for 2 minutes until softened but not browned. Add the turkey and brown on all sides, stirring. Add the remaining ingredients except the potatoes.

2. Cover with the lid and bring up to High pressure, then reduce the heat and cook for 6 minutes.

3. Remove from the heat and reduce the pressure quickly under cold water.

4. Stir the goulash, taste and re-season. Add a little extra stock or water if necessary. Add the potatoes.

5. Cover with the lid, bring back to High pressure and cook for a further 4 minutes.

6. Reduce the pressure quickly under cold water again.

7. Stir gently. Spoon into bowls and serve garnished with soured cream or crème fraîche and a sprinkling of chopped parsley.

This is usually cooked on a trivet in the oven for a long time to make it meltingly tender. Here it is cooked really quickly in the pressure cooker. The difference is that the skin isn't used, making it a much healthier option. For a more substantial meal, use flour tortillas instead of the tiny Chinese pancakes – it saves a lot of effort having to roll so many and is really tasty.

Serves 4 | Preparation time: 15 minutes, plus marinating | Cooking time: 30 minutes

Melting Peking Duck

4 duck leg portions

2 tbsp soy sauce

2 tsp grated fresh root ginger

1 garlic clove, chopped

1 tsp Chinese five-spice powder

1 tbsp clear honey

450ml water

1 tbsp lemon juice

To serve

24 Chinese pancakes

Hoisin sauce

1 bunch of spring onions, shredded

¼–½ cucumber, cut into thin strips

1. Remove as much skin as possible from the duck and make several slashes in the meat. Blend together all the remaining ingredients except the water and lemon juice in a shallow dish. Add the duck and coat completely in the marinade. Cover and chill for at least 2 hours, if time.

2. Put the water and lemon juice in the cooker. Line the steamer basket with foil. Arrange the duck and any remaining marinade on the foil. Place on the trivet in the pressure cooker.

3. Cover with the lid and bring up to High pressure, then reduce the heat and cook for 30 minutes.

4. Remove from the heat and allow the pressure to reduce slowly at room temperature.

5. Lift the duck out of the basket and pull all the meat off the bones - it should fall off easily. Discard the bones, then shred the meat between two forks.

6. Meanwhile warm the pancakes according to the packet directions.

7. To serve, smear each pancake with a little hoisin sauce, add some meat and a little spring onion and cucumber. Roll up and enjoy.

I love dried blueberries but you could use raisins, cranberries or chopped apricots instead, if you prefer. Pistachios are expensive but do taste wonderful, although you could use almonds instead, which are less costly. You can just leave pre-cooked couscous to soak in boiling stock or water but here, as it has extra ingredients, I've mixed it and put it in the pressure cooker to finish cooking.

Serves 4 | Preparation time: 10 minutes | Cooking time: 14 minutes

Duck with Dried Blueberries and Mushrooms on Pistachio Couscous

1 tbsp olive oil

2 large skinless duck breasts, cut into bite-sized pieces

12 button onions, peeled but left whole

1 large garlic clove, crushed

2 large carrots, peeled and chopped

550ml hot chicken stock

1 tsp ground cumin

50g dried blueberries

2 beefsteak tomatoes, skinned and chopped

225g couscous

1 courgette, finely chopped

50g shelled pistachios

1 tbsp cornflour

1 tbsp water

2 tbsp chopped fresh mint

To serve

Rocket salad

1. Heat the oil in the pressure cooker. Add the duck and brown quickly, stirring all the time. Remove the duck with a slotted spoon and reserve. Add the onions, garlic and carrots and fry for 2 minutes, stirring. Add 300ml of the stock and all the remaining ingredients except the mint, cornflour, couscous, water, courgette and pistachios. Return the duck to the pan.

2. Cover with the lid and bring up to High pressure, then reduce the heat and cook for 8 minutes.

3. Remove from the heat and reduce the pressure quickly under cold water.

4. Meanwhile, mix the couscous with the courgette and pistachios in a heatproof bowl that will fit in the pressure cooker. Stir the remaining stock into the couscous. Put the bowl in the pressure cooker, bring back up to High pressure, reduce the heat and cook for 2 minutes.

5. Remove from the heat and reduce the pressure quickly under cold water.

6. Carefully lift out the couscous and keep it warm. Blend the cornflour with the water and stir into the pressure cooker with the mint. Cook in the open cooker, stirring, for 1 minute until thickened and clear. Taste and re-season.

7. Fluff up the couscous, then spoon it onto plates and spoon the duck over. Serve with a rocket salad.

Duck with orange is a classic combination that can't be beaten. For a special meal, it's worth bothering to segment the orange to use as a garnish but it isn't vital so omit that stage if you prefer. Crusty bread and a watercress salad are the perfect accompaniments, or you could serve it with new potatoes.

Serves 4 | Preparation time: 10 minutes | Cooking time: 10 minutes

Braised Duck with Orange

A large knob of butter

4 duck leg portions

2 onions, chopped

100g baby button mushrooms

2 tsp chopped fresh thyme

300ml chicken stock

150ml orange juice

Salt and freshly ground black pepper

2 tsp tomato purée

½ tsp caster sugar

4 tbsp plain flour

To garnish

1 orange, segmented

2 tbsp chopped fresh parsley

1. Heat the butter in the pressure cooker and fry the duck for 2 minutes until browned. Lift out with a slotted spoon and reserve. Add the onions and fry, stirring, for 2 minutes until lightly browned. Add the mushrooms, thyme, stock and all but 100ml of the orange juice. Season with salt and pepper and stir in the tomato purée and sugar. Return the duck to the pan.

2. Cover with the lid and bring up to High pressure, then reduce the heat and cook for 10 minutes.

3. Remove from the heat and reduce the pressure quickly under cold water.

4. Carefully lift the duck out of the pan and keep it warm. Blend the flour with the remaining orange juice and stir it into the pan. Bring to the boil and cook for 2 minutes, stirring until thickened. Taste and re-season.

5. Serve the duck garnished with the orange segments and chopped parsley.

A special-occasion casserole, this makes a delicious dish. Pheasant can be very dry when roasted so I prefer to pressure cook it in a sweet and sharp sauce to render it wonderfully tender. If you like, you could add some baby potatoes after 8 minutes then re-cover with the lid, bring back to pressure and cook for 4 minutes.

Serves 2–4 | Preparation time: 10 minutes | Cooking time: 16 minutes

Casserole of Pheasant with Cider and Pears

A large knob of butter

1 pheasant, halved or quartered, depending on size

1 onion, chopped

1 celery stick, chopped

2 firm pears, peeled, cored and diced

150ml medium-dry cider

150ml chicken stock

1/2 tsp dried mixed herbs

Salt and freshly ground black pepper

2 tbsp plain flour

2 tbsp water

To garnish

A handful of watercress

To serve

Warm ciabatta bread

Mixed green salad

1. Rinse the pheasant and pat dry on kitchen paper. Melt the butter in the pressure cooker and fry the pheasant until browned, then remove and set aside. Add the onion and celery and fry for 2 minutes, stirring. Return the pheasant to the pan flesh-sides down, and add the pears, cider, stock and mixed herbs. Season well with salt and pepper.

2. Cover with the lid and bring up to High pressure, then reduce the heat and cook for 12 minutes.

3. Remove from the heat and reduce the pressure quickly under cold water.

4. Lift out the pheasant, transfer to serving plates and keep warm. Blend the flour with the water and stir into the sauce. Bring to the boil and boil for 2 minutes, stirring all the time. Taste and re-season.

5. Spoon the sauce over the pheasant, garnish with watercress and serve with warm ciabatta and a green salad.

Pheasant, beetroot and fennel go remarkably well together and make a delicious dish. The slightly gamey flavour of the pheasant is complemented by the sweet earthiness of the beetroot and the aniseed taste of the fennel. Cut the potatoes small so they are really soft for mashing.

Serves 4 | Preparation time: 10 minutes | Cooking time: 25 minutes

Pheasant with Baby Beetroot and Fennel

40g butter

1 cock pheasant, quartered

1 red onion, chopped

1 head of fennel, trimmed and sliced

Salt and freshly ground black pepper

8 cooked baby beetroot, peeled and quartered

8 juniper berries, lightly crushed

4 tbsp Pernod (or other pastis)

200ml chicken stock

1 tbsp tomato purée

2 tbsp cornflour

900g potatoes, peeled and cut into small chunks

A splash of milk

To garnish

A small handful of chopped fresh parsley

To serve

Shredded kale

1. Heat a good knob of the butter in the pressure cooker and brown the pheasant on all sides. Remove from the pan and set aside.

2. Heat half the remaining butter, add the onion and fennel to the pan and cook, stirring, for 2 minutes. Add all the remaining ingredients except the potatoes and milk. Return the pheasant to the pan, skin-sides down.

3. Cover with the lid and bring up to High pressure, then reduce the heat and cook for 10 minutes.

4. Remove from the heat and reduce the pressure quickly under cold water.

5. Put the potatoes in the steaming basket and add it to the pan. Re-cover with the lid, bring back to High pressure, reduce the heat and cook for 4 minutes.

6. Remove from the heat and reduce the pressure quickly under cold water.

7. Tip the potatoes into a bowl. Mash well with the remaining butter, a splash of milk and salt and pepper to taste. Keep warm.

8. Carefully lift out the pheasant, beetroot and fennel and keep them warm. Boil the cooking liquid rapidly in the open pan for a couple of minutes until reduced and slightly thickened. Taste and re-season, if necessary.

9. Pile the mash on plates. Top with the pheasant, beetroot and fennel. Spoon the sauce over, sprinkle with parsley and serve with kale.

Guinea fowl is much like a small chicken but with a bit more of a gamey flavour. I particularly like it casseroled as it can be a bit dry if roasted (unless you bard the breast well with fat bacon first). It is therefore the perfect candidate for the pressure cooker treatment.

Serves 4 | Preparation time: 20 minutes | Cooking time: 20 minutes

Guinea Fowl in Cider with Pork Belly

1 guinea fowl, quartered

Salt and freshly ground black pepper

250g belly pork rashers, rinded and diced

12 button onions, peeled but left whole

50g butter

2 tbsp brandy

150ml medium-dry cider

150ml chicken stock

1 bouquet garni sachet

1 tsp soft light brown sugar

100g crimini or white button mushrooms, left whole

400g baby potatoes, scrubbed

250g baby carrots, peeled and trimmed

100g baby corn, cut into thirds

3 tbsp plain flour

3 tbsp water

To garnish

Chopped fresh parsley

1. Season the guinea fowl joints with salt and pepper. Fry the pork in the pressure cooker until the fat runs and the pork is beginning to brown, tossing all the time. Remove from the pan with a slotted spoon. Add the onions and brown in the pork fat. Remove from the pan and set aside. Melt about a quarter of the butter in the pan and brown the guinea fowl on all sides., finishing skin-sides down. Return the pork to the pan. Add the brandy and cider, the stock, bouquet garni, sugar, mushrooms and a little salt and pepper.

2. Cover with the lid and bring up to High pressure, then reduce the heat and cook for 8 minutes.

3. Remove from the heat and reduce the pressure quickly under cold water.

4. Add the button onions to the guinea fowl. Put the prepared vegetables in the steaming basket and put it on top of the guinea fowl.

5. Cover with the lid and bring back to High pressure, then cook for 4 minutes.

6. Reduce the pressure quickly under cold water again.

7. Lift out the vegetables and keep warm. Remove the guinea fowl, onions and mushrooms with a slotted spoon and keep warm as well. Discard the bouquet garni.

8. Mash the remaining butter and the flour together until smooth. Gradually whisk the butter mixture into the liquid in the pan over a medium heat until thickened and smooth. Continue cooking for 2 minutes, stirring all the time. Taste and re-season, if necessary. Return the onions and mushrooms to the sauce. Spoon the sauce over the guinea fowl on plates. Sprinkle with chopped parsley and serve with the baby vegetables.

The addition of anchovies is a Victorian tradition to enrich meat sauces, in the same way Asians use fish sauces. It doesn't taste fishy but simply delicious! I always keep a tube of paste in the fridge to add amazing depth of flavour to soups, stews and casseroles.

Serves 4 | Preparation time: 20 minutes | Cooking time: 25 minutes

Rich Venison Casserole with Butternut Squash

2 tbsp olive oil

700g diced venison

1 celery stick, chopped

1 onion, chopped

2 carrots, peeled and sliced

50g smoked bacon lardons

1 garlic clove, crushed

400g can of chopped tomatoes

100ml beef stock

100ml red wine

1 tbsp tomato purée

2 tsp anchovy paste

1 bouquet garni

½ tsp caster sugar

100g crimini mushrooms, wiped but left whole

Salt and freshly ground black pepper

1 small butternut squash, cut into small chunks

16 baby waxy potatoes, scrubbed

3 tbsp plain flour

3 tbsp water

To garnish

A small handful of chopped parsley

To serve

Watercress salad

1. Heat half the oil in the pressure cooker. Add the venison and brown all over. Remove from the cooker.

2. Heat the remaining oil and fry the onion, carrot, celery, lardons and garlic, stirring, for 2–3 minutes until the vegetables are softening and lightly golden. Return the venison to the pan and add all the remaining ingredients except the squash, potatoes, flour and water. Season well with salt and pepper.

3. Cover with the lid and bring up to High pressure, then reduce the heat and cook for 16 minutes.

4. Remove from the heat and reduce the pressure quickly under cold water.

5. Open the cooker and spread the squash over the surface. Put the potatoes in the steaming basket and put on top of the squash. Sprinkle lightly with salt, if liked. Re-cover with the lid and bring back to High pressure, then reduce the heat and cook for 4 minutes.

6. Remove from the heat and reduce the pressure quickly again under cold water.

7. Lift out the potatoes and keep them warm. Blend the flour and water together and gently stir into the pan, taking care not to break up the squash too much. Bring to the boil in the open cooker and simmer for 2 minutes, stirring gently until thickened. Taste and re-season, if necessary.

8. Sprinkle the venison with the chopped parsley and serve with the potatoes and a watercress salad.

Rabbit is delicious – it tastes very much like chicken and is worth a try even if you've never cooked it before. This is just a simple casserole which I like to serve with rice and a leafy green salad but you could throw extra carrots into the pot and cook some broccoli or green beans separately.

Serves 4–6 | Preparation time: 15 minutes | Cooking time: 15 minutes

Creamy Rabbit Stew

1 rabbit, jointed

Salt and freshly ground black pepper

A knob of butter

1 tbsp sunflower oil

50g unsmoked bacon lardons

2 onions, halved and sliced

2 large carrots, peeled and thickly sliced

1 large parsnip, diced

250ml chicken stock

1 bouquet garni sachet

4 tbsp crème fraîche

To garnish

2 tbsp chopped fresh parsley

1. Season the rabbit pieces with salt and pepper. Melt the butter and oil in the pressure cooker and brown the rabbit joints, then remove from the pan. Add the lardons and onions and fry gently, stirring, for 2 minutes until lightly browned. Pour off any excess fat. Add the remaining vegetables and return the rabbit to the pan. Add the stock and bouquet garni.

2. Cover with the lid and bring up to High pressure, then reduce the heat and cook for 13 minutes.

3. Remove from the heat and reduce the pressure quickly under cold water.

4. Carefully lift out the rabbit and carrots (the parsnip will probably have 'melted' into the liquid pretty much). Discard the bouquet garni. Boil the liquid rapidly for 2 minutes in the open pan until reduced slightly, then stir in the crème fraîche. Return the rabbit and carrots to the pan and reheat briefly. Taste and re-season.

5. Serve garnished with the chopped parsley.

Chapter 13

Vegetarian

Cooking vegetables, particularly hard ones like roots and tubers, takes quite a while on the hob or in the oven, but in the pressure cooker it is very quick indeed. Cooking pulses is also speeded up considerably and you don't have to boil for 10 minutes first to destroy toxins – that happens during the pressure cooking as the temperature is raised sufficiently to kill them. Here you'll find a whole array of delicious vegetarian meals, all well balanced and packed with flavour and goodness that can be cooked in a fraction of the time it would take cooking conventionally.

The smoked paprika adds an almost 'meaty' flavour to the ragout and enriches it enormously. All you need to serve it with is some good crusty bread and a crisp green salad. You can use two large cans of chickpeas and start at step 5 if time is short.

Serves 4 | Preparation time: 15 minutes | Cooking time: 36 minutes

Chickpea, Sweet Potato and Aubergine Ragout with Smoked Paprika

225g chickpeas, soaked in cold water for several hours or overnight

2 tbsp olive oil

1 large onion, chopped

1 large aubergine, diced

1 sweet potato, about 350g, peeled and diced

1 yellow pepper, diced

1 red pepper, diced

1 garlic clove, crushed

2 tsp smoked paprika

1 tbsp sweet paprika

400g can of chopped tomatoes

2 tbsp tomato purée

150ml vegetable stock

1 bay leaf

Salt and freshly ground black pepper

To garnish

4 tbsp soured cream

2 tbsp chopped fresh parsley

1. Put the drained chickpeas in the pressure cooker and just cover with water. Bring to the boil and skim off any scum that rises to the surface. Reduce the heat to medium.

2. Cover with the lid and bring up to High pressure over a medium heat, then reduce the heat and cook for 25 minutes.

3. Remove from the heat and allow the pressure to reduce slowly at room temperature.

4. Drain the chickpeas and rinse and dry the pressure cooker.

5. Heat the oil in the cooker. Add the onion and fry, stirring, for 2 minutes to soften. Add the aubergine, sweet potato and peppers and cook, stirring, for 2 minutes. Stir in the drained chickpeas and all the remaining ingredients, and season with salt and pepper.

6. Cover with the lid and bring up to High pressure, then reduce the heat and cook for 5 minutes.

7. Remove from the heat and reduce the pressure quickly under cold water.

8. Remove the lid and boil rapidly to reduce the liquid so everything is bathed in a rich sauce. Taste and re-season, if necessary. Spoon into bowls and garnish each with a dollop of soured cream and a sprinkling of parsley.

I like to serve this with some halved baby plum tomatoes and chives tossed in French dressing as a refreshing accompaniment that cuts through the richness of the sauce. You can cook the pasta in a separate pan according to the packet directions whilst making the stroganoff if you prefer, and use two cans of beans and start at the fourth step for quickness.

Serves 4 | Preparation time: 20 minutes, plus soaking | Cooking time: 24 minutes

Onion and Butter Bean Stroganoff with Wilted Spinach Noodles

225g butter beans, soaked in cold water for several hours or overnight

400g green tagliatelle

Boiling water

Salt and freshly ground black pepper

75g butter

4 large white onions, halved and thinly sliced

2 tbsp brandy

400ml soured cream

2 tbsp chopped fresh parsley

3 tbsp chopped fresh dill

2 tbsp cornflour

2 tbsp milk

400g spinach, well washed and drained

Freshly grated nutmeg

To garnish

A little chopped fresh parsley

1. Drain the beans and put them in the pressure cooker. Cover with plenty of water (but make sure the cooker is no more than one-third full). Bring to the boil, then reduce the heat to medium. Cover with the lid and bring up to High pressure over a medium heat, then cook for 15 minutes.

2. Remove from the heat and allow the pressure to reduce slowly at room temperature. Drain the beans and set aside.

3. Put the tagliatelle in the cooker. Cover with plenty of boiling water but make sure it is no more than half full, and add a good pinch of salt. Cover with the lid and bring up to High pressure, then reduce the heat and cook for 3 minutes.

4. Remove from the heat and allow the pressure to reduce slowly at room temperature. Drain the tagliatelle in a colander and set aside.

5. Melt 50g of the butter in the pressure cooker. Add the onions and cook, stirring, for 3 minutes until softening and browning slightly. Return the beans to the pan and stir in the brandy, soured cream and herbs. Blend the cornflour with the milk and stir in with some salt and pepper. Cover with the lid and bring up to High pressure, then reduce the heat and cook for 3 minutes.

6. Remove from the heat and reduce the pressure quickly under cold water. Stir well, taste and re-season, if necessary.

7. Meanwhile, put the spinach in a separate pan and cook, tossing gently, for about 3 minutes until wilted. Drain thoroughly, chop, then return to the pan with the remaining butter.

8. Pour boiling water over the tagliatelle to heat and loosen it, then drain it and add it to the spinach and toss until well mixed. Season with salt, pepper and plenty of grated nutmeg. Pile the spinach noodles on plates and spoon the stroganoff over the top. Sprinkle with parsley and serve.

These make a delicious starter, side dish or lunch and are really simple to make. Ring the changes with other roots when in season. They have a Greek-style flavour so try them topped with some crumbled feta cheese and a few chopped olives too.

Serves 4–8 | Preparation time: 25 minutes | Cooking time: 8 minutes

Couscous-stuffed Cabbage Leaves with Carrots, Currants and Pine Nuts

1 large carrot, peeled and coarsely grated

1 small onion, grated

1 garlic clove, crushed

75g bulgur

50g toasted pine nuts

50g currants

1 tsp dried oregano

1 tsp ground cinnamon

Salt and freshly ground black pepper

8 large green cabbage leaves

600ml vegetable stock

3 tbsp tomato purée

2 bay leaves

To serve

Crusty bread

1. Mix the carrots with the onion, garlic, bulgur, pine nuts, currants, oregano and cinnamon. Season well with salt and pepper.

2. Cut out the thick central stalks from the cabbage leaves. Plunge the leaves into boiling water for 2 minutes. Drain, rinse with cold water and drain again. Dry the leaves on kitchen paper.

3. Divide the stuffing amongst the leaves. Fold over the points where the stalks were, then fold in the sides and roll up the leaves, not too tightly to allow for the couscous expanding, to form parcels. Pack side by side in the pressure cooker. Mix the stock with the tomato purée and pour over. Tuck in the bay leaves.

4. Cover with the lid and bring up to High pressure, then reduce the heat and cook for 8 minutes.

5. Remove from the heat and allow the pressure to reduce slowly at room temperature.

6. Discard the bay leaves and carefully lift out the cabbage rolls. Taste the juices and re-season, if necessary. Serve the rolls with the juices spooned over and with plenty of crusty bread.

You can make this just with two kinds of beans – I like butter beans and black eye beans but using this colourful mix adds depth and flavour. You could use two cans of mixed pulses and at step 5 – there will be slightly fewer beans but it won't matter much!

Serves 4 | Preparation time: 15 minutes, plus soaking | Cooking time: 33 minutes

Spiced Mixed Bean Stew with Shredded Greens

250g mixed dried bean mix, soaked in cold water for several hours or overnight

2 tbsp olive oil

1 bunch of spring onions, chopped

2 garlic cloves, chopped

1 tsp ground turmeric

1 tsp ground cumin

1/4 tsp ground cloves

750ml vegetable stock

1/2 small celeriac, diced

1 large carrot, peeled and diced

1 bay leaf

Freshly ground black pepper

250g spring greens or kale, finely shredded, discarding thick stumps

2 courgettes, cut into thin ribbons with a potato peeler

2 tbsp chopped fresh parsley

2 tbsp chopped fresh coriander or basil

2 tbsp tahini paste

150ml crème fraîche

A dash of lime juice

1. Drain the beans and place them in the pressure cooker. Cover with cold water so the cooker is no more than one-third full. Bring to the boil in the open cooker and skim off any scum that rises to the surface. Reduce the heat to medium and bring to a gentle simmer.

2. Cover with the lid and bring up to High pressure, then reduce the heat and cook for 20 minutes.

3. Remove from the heat and allow the pressure to reduce slowly at room temperature.

4. Drain the beans and set aside. Rinse out the pressure cooker.

5. Heat the oil in the cooker, add the spring onions and fry, stirring, for 1 minute. Add the garlic, turmeric, cumin and cloves and fry for 30 seconds. Stir in the stock and prepared vegetables. Add the bay leaf, a little salt and a good grinding of black pepper.

6. Cover with the lid, bring back up to High pressure, reduce the heat and cook for 5 minutes.

7. Remove from the heat and reduce the pressure quickly under cold water.

8. Add the greens and the cooked dried beans, stir and bring back to the boil in the open cooker. Reduce the heat and simmer for a further 3 minutes, stirring once or twice.

9. Stir in the courgettes and simmer a further 2 minutes until everything is really tender. Discard the bay leaf. Gently stir in the herbs, tahini paste and all but 4 tsp of the crème fraîche (reserve the rest for garnish). Sharpen to taste with lime juice and re-season, if necessary. Ladle into warm bowls and top each with a small dollop of crème fraîche.

This is almost an old-style vegetarian recipe using a sort of nut roast mixture but it's really tasty and very quick to make. You can also use the same mixture to stuff eight courgettes or cup-shaped portabello mushrooms.

Serves 4 | Preparation time: 15 minutes | Cooking time: 7 minutes

Peanut-stuffed Peppers with Cheese and Herby Tomato Sauce

225g roasted unsalted peanuts, chopped

100g fresh breadcrumbs

1 small onion, grated

1 tbsp soy sauce

1 tsp dried oregano

A large knob of butter

2 tsp Marmite or other yeast extract

120ml boiling water

4 large red peppers

75g Cheddar cheese, grated

250ml vegetable stock

2 tbsp tomato purée

2 tbsp chopped fresh basil

Salt and freshly ground black pepper

To serve

Crusty bread

Mixed green salad

1. Mix together the nuts, breadcrumbs, onion, soy sauce and oregano. Blend together the butter, Marmite and the boiling water until melted. Stir into the nut mixture until it is thoroughly blended.

2. Cut the peppers in halves and remove the seeds. Pack the nut mixture into the peppers. Pile the cheese on top.

3. Put the stock in the pressure cooker. Add 4 pepper halves to the cooker, stuffing-sides up (they should be in liquid but not submerged). Put the trivet in the cooker, lay the other 4 halves in the steamer basket and place on the trivet.

4. Cover with the lid and bring up to High pressure, then reduce the heat and cook for 5 minutes.

5. Remove from the heat and reduce the pressure quickly under cold water.

6. Remove the basket and the trivet from the pressure cooker. Carefully lift out the remaining 4 pepper halves with a slotted spoon. Place the peppers on serving plates. Stir the tomato purée into the stock. Bring to the boil in the open cooker and simmer, stirring, until slightly thickened.

7. Stir in the basil and season to taste with salt and pepper. Spoon the sauce over the peppers and serve hot with crusty bread and a green salad.

Couscous just lends itself to the Middle Eastern flavours of cinnamon, cumin and ginger. It also goes perfectly with firm, salty halloumi and sweet, soft butternut squash, making this the perfect vegetarian supper dish.

Serves 4 | Preparation time: 15 minutes | Cooking time: 12 minutes

Couscous with Butternut Squash and Halloumi Cheese

A large knob of butter

1 onion, chopped

1 garlic clove, crushed

1 turnip diced

½ small swede, diced

1 small butternut squash, diced

Salt and freshly ground black pepper

1 tsp ground cumin

½ tsp ground cinnamon

½ tsp ground ginger

250ml vegetable stock

225g couscous

250g block of halloumi cheese, diced

A handful of black olives, stoned

2 tbsp chopped fresh coriander

A little olive oil

1. Melt the butter in the pressure cooker. Add the vegetables and fry, stirring, for 2 minutes. Add the spices and a little salt and pepper, toss well, then add the stock.

2. Cover with the lid and bring up to High pressure, then reduce the heat and cook for 3 minutes.

3. Remove from the heat and reduce the pressure quickly under cold water.

4. Strain the vegetables, reserving the liquid. Stir the stock into the couscous in a heatproof bowl and leave to stand for 5 minutes. Meanwhile, return the vegetables to the pressure cooker and add the halloumi.

5. Cover with the lid and seal it. Leave for 4 minutes until the couscous has soaked, then open the cooker and add the couscous to the vegetables and cheese with the olives and coriander. Toss gently over a low heat until piping hot. Spoon onto plates and drizzle with a little olive oil before serving.

This is a wonderful mixture of vegetables, cheese and eggs bathed in a rich curry sauce. The eggs are cooked in the pressure cooker in a non-perforated separator. If you don't have one, put them in a small heatproof bowl that will fit at one side of the cooker.

Serves 4 | Preparation time: 10 minutes | Cooking time: 10 minutes

Paneer, Egg and Vegetable Madras

4 eggs

2 tbsp sunflower oil

1 large onion chopped

1 garlic clove, crushed

3 tbsp Madras curry powder or paste

2 carrots, peeled and thickly sliced

2 potatoes, cut into bite-sized chunks

1/2 small swede, cut into bite-sized chunks

1/2 tsp salt

1/4 tsp chilli powder

3 tomatoes, chopped

400ml can thick coconut milk

2 tbsp tomato purée

2 tbsp mango chutney

2 tbsp chopped fresh coriander, plus extra to garnish

250g block of paneer, diced

100g mangetout

To serve

Naan bread

Mango chutney

1. Scrub the eggs, wrap each one in kitchen foil and place in a non-perforated separator.

2. Heat the oil in the pressure cooker. Add the onion and fry, stirring, for 3 minutes until softened and lightly golden. Add the garlic and curry powder or paste and fry for 30 seconds. Stir in all the remaining ingredients except the mangetout. Make a space at the side of the cooker and add the container with the eggs.

3. Cover with the lid and bring up to High pressure, then reduce the heat and cook for 4 minutes.

4. Remove from the heat and reduce the pressure quickly under cold water. Lift out the container of eggs and immediately cover with cold water.

5. Add the mangetout to the curry and boil in the open cooker for 2–3 minutes until tender and the sauce is rich and thick, stirring gently occasionally. Taste and re-season, if necessary. Shell and halve the eggs.

6. Spoon the curry into bowls and top each with 2 halves of egg. Serve hot with naan bread and mango chutney.

When baby aubergines are available they are perfect for this, simply use eight, trimmed and cut into halves. You could also substitute a small sweet potato for the ordinary one. Try it with baby courgettes instead of aubergine.

Serves 4 | Preparation time: 10 minutes | Cooking time: 10 minutes

Aubergine, Pea and Lentil Curry

100g brown or green lentils

3 tbsp sunflower oil

1 onion, chopped

1 garlic clove, crushed

1 large waxy potato, scrubbed and diced

1 large aubergine, cut into thick batons

1 tsp ground cumin

1 tsp ground coriander

1 tsp ground turmeric

$\frac{1}{2}$ tsp chilli powder

$\frac{1}{4}$ tsp ground cloves

100ml vegetable stock

150ml thick plain yoghurt

225g frozen peas

Salt and freshly ground black pepper

2 tbsp chopped fresh coriander

To serve

Naan bread

Lime pickle

1. Put the lentils in the pressure cooker. Cover with plenty of water but make sure the cooker is no more than one-third full. Bring to the boil in the open cooker. Reduce the heat to medium.

2. Cover with the lid and bring up to High pressure over a medium heat, then reduce the heat and cook for 3 minutes.

3. Remove from the heat and allow the pressure to reduce slowly at room temperature. Drain and set aside. Rinse and dry the cooker.

4. Heat the oil in the pressure cooker and fry the onion for 2 minutes. Add the garlic, potato, aubergine and spices and cook, stirring, for 1 minute. Add all the remaining ingredients except the coriander, including the lentils. Stir well.

5. Cover with the lid, bring back to High pressure, reduce the heat and cook for 5 minutes.

6. Remove from the heat and reduce the pressure quickly under cold water.

7. Taste and add more salt and pepper if necessary. Stir in the coriander. Serve hot with naan bread and lime pickle.

Brown rice is good in a pressure cooker as it is less likely to become too soft if overcooked. You could also substitute half wild rice for half the brown for a nice change. To crush the coriander, if you don't have a pestle and mortar, put it in a small bowl and use the end of a rolling pin.

Serves 4 | Preparation time: 10 minutes | Cooking time: 11 minutes

Brown Rice, Mushroom and Pistachio Pilaf

2 tbsp sunflower oil

1 tsp roughly crushed coriander seeds

1 tsp cumin seeds

1 onion, chopped

2 garlic cloves, crushed

250g chestnut mushrooms, sliced

2 tsp grated fresh root ginger

200g long grain brown rice

100g toasted pistachios

2 tsp garam masala

500ml hot vegetable stock

1 bay leaf

Freshly ground black pepper

To garnish

2 tbsp chopped fresh coriander or parsley

4 lemon wedges

To serve

1 avocado, peeled, stoned and chopped

Cucumber and spring onion salad dressed simply with olive oil and lime juice

1. Heat the oil in the pressure cooker. Add the seeds and fry for 30 seconds until fragrant. Add the onion and garlic and fry, stirring, for 3 minutes until softened and lightly golden. Stir in the mushrooms, ginger, rice, nuts and garam masala and cook, stirring, for 30 seconds. Pour in the hot stock, add the bay leaf and plenty of black pepper. Bring to the boil and stir well. Reduce the heat to medium.

2. Cover with the lid and bring up to High pressure over a medium heat, then reduce the heat and cook for 7 minutes.

3. Remove from the heat and allow the pressure to reduce slowly at room temperature.

4. Open the cooker and, if necessary, boil rapidly in the open cooker to remove any remaining liquid. Taste and re-season, if necessary.

5. Garnish with the chopped coriander or parsley and lemon wedges and serve with the chopped avocado sprinkled over a cucumber an spring onion salad.

This is also delicious served cold, when the flavours develop even more. Simply dress the cold lentils and vegetables with a little balsamic vinegar to taste and drizzle the whole thing with a little extra virgin olive oil.

Serves 4 | Preparation time: 15 minutes | Cooking time: 5 minutes

Puy Lentil and Vegetable Pot with Griddled Halloumi

175g puy lentils

2 carrots, cut into small dice

8 radishes, trimmed and halved

1 red pepper, cut into small dice

2 courgettes, cut into small dice

4 spring onions, chopped

300ml vegetable stock

90ml white wine

1 bay leaf

Salt and freshly ground black pepper

2 tbsp chopped fresh parsley

250g block halloumi, cut into 8 slices

2 tbsp olive oil

2 tbsp chopped fresh thyme

1. Rinse the lentils and place in the pressure cooker. Add the vegetables, stock, wine and bay leaf. Bring to the boil, then reduce the heat to medium.

2. Cover with the lid and bring up to High pressure, then reduce the heat and cook for 3 minutes.

3. Remove from the heat and allow the pressure to reduce slowly at room temperature.

4. Discard the bay leaf. Stir well. Boil rapidly in the open cooker to remove any excess liquid. Season to taste with salt and pepper and stir in the parsley.

5. Meanwhile, preheat a griddle pan and drizzle with a little oil (it must be oiled or the cheese will stick). Brush the halloumi with the oil and sprinkle all over with the thyme. Griddle the cheese for 1 minute on each side, pressing down with a fish slice until striped brown and hot through.

6. Spoon the lentils and vegetables into bowls and top with the halloumi to serve.

This is a favourite of mine and is ideal for cooking in the pressure cooker. Use sweet potato or pumpkin instead of butternut squash, if you prefer. You can even use ripe marrow but its flavour won't be as sweet. Garnish with Crispy Sage (see page 38).

Serves 4 | Preparation time: 10 minutes | Cooking time: 20 minutes

Butternut Squash and Blue Cheese Orzotto

2 tbsp olive oil

1 bunch of spring onions, chopped, reserving some green for garnish

1 garlic clove, crushed

300g pearl barley

900ml vegetable stock

Salt and freshly ground black pepper

1 small butternut squash (about 650g), cut into large dice

2 tbsp chopped fresh sage

6 tbsp crème fraîche

150g creamy blue cheese, like Dolcelatte or Castello

To serve

A mixed salad

1. Heat the oil in the pressure cooker. Add the spring onions and garlic and cook, stirring, for 2 minutes until softened but not browned. Add the barley and stir well. Add the stock and season with salt and a good grinding of pepper. Bring back to the boil, then reduce the heat to medium.

2. Cover with the lid and bring up to High pressure over a medium heat, then reduce the heat and cook for 10 minutes.

3. Remove from the heat and reduce the pressure quickly under cold water.

4. Add the squash and sage. Bring back to High pressure, reduce the heat and cook for a further 10 minutes.

5. Remove from the heat and allow the pressure to reduce slowly at room temperature.

6. Gently fold in the crème fraîche and blue cheese, re-cover and leave to stand for 3 minutes.

7. Spoon the orzotto into warm bowls and garnish with the reserved chopped green spring onion to serve.

This is delicious served with a crisp salad as a light meal or as a starter in smaller quantities. It can also be served as an accompaniment to grilled meat or fish, very simple but beautiful. Time carefully for a nutty but creamy result.

Serves 4 | Preparation time: 10 minutes | Cooking time: 5 minutes

All-in-one Risotto Milanese

2 tbsp olive oil

1 onion, finely chopped

350g risotto rice

1 litre boiling vegetable stock

A good pinch of saffron strands

Salt and freshly ground black pepper

1 small bay leaf

25g unsalted butter

2 tbsp grated Parmesan cheese

To garnish

A little chopped fresh parsley

A few Parmesan shavings

1. Heat the oil in the pressure cooker. Add the onion and fry gently, stirring, for 3 minutes until softened but not browned.

2. Stir in the rice and cook for 1 minute, stirring, until glistening with oil.

3. Add the stock, saffron, a little salt and pepper and the bay leaf. Bring back to the boil stirring. Reduce the heat to medium.

4. Cover with the lid, bring up to High pressure over a medium heat, then reduce the heat and cook for 5 minutes.

5. Remove from the heat and allow the pressure to reduce slowly at room temperature.

6. Stir in the butter and grated Parmesan. The rice should be creamy with still a little texture. Taste and re-season, if necessary. Discard the bay leaf. Spoon into bowls and garnish with chopped parsley and a few Parmesan shavings.

Chapter 14

Side Dishes and Accompaniments

The pressure cooker can hold you in good stead when you are cooking simple main courses liked grilled chops, poached fish or fried chicken or when you're using the microwave oven, even the barbecue. Of course, any quick to cook mains require quick to cook accompaniments so all of these ideas take only minutes to make. Throughout the book I have often told you how to cook the accompaniment at the same time as the main meal but these are for the times when you aren't using the cooker for the rest of the dish.

The great thing about cooking potatoes in the pressure cooker is they become uniformly soft so no lumpy bits in the finished mash as long as you cut them in even-sized pieces. These are delicious with cold meats, grills, or rich casseroles.

Serves 4 | Preparation time: 7 minutes | Cooking time: 7 minutes | Vegetarian

Creamy Garlic Mash

1kg floury potatoes, peeled and cut into even-sized chunky pieces

300ml water

Salt and freshly ground black pepper

25g butter

4 tbsp single cream

1 garlic clove, crushed

1. Put the potatoes in the pressure cooker with the water and a large pinch of salt.

2. Cover with the lid and bring up to High pressure, then reduce the heat and cook for 5 minutes.

3. Remove from the heat and reduce the pressure quickly under cold water. Test that the potatoes are really soft.

4. Drain the potatoes thoroughly, then return to the pan. Cook over a low heat for 1–2 minutes, stirring to dry. Remove from the heat.

5. Add the butter, cream and garlic and mash thoroughly with a potato masher, then beat with the masher or a wooden spoon until fluffy and smooth. Season with more salt, if necessary, and lots of pepper.

These are gorgeous served with dishes like fried chicken, grilled sausages or poached fish. I've discovered recently that packs of grated cheese are often no more expensive than buying the block so are worth keeping in the fridge for cooking – it saves all that bother!

Serves 4 | Preparation time: 7 minutes | Cooking time: 7 minutes | Vegetarian

Fluffy Cheese Potatoes

1kg floury potatoes, peeled and cut into even-sized chunky pieces

300ml water

Salt and freshly ground black pepper

25g butter, plus extra to serve (optional)

4 tbsp milk

75g strong Cheddar cheese, grated

1. Put the potatoes in the pressure cooker with the water and a large pinch of salt.

2. Cover with the lid and bring up to High pressure, then reduce the heat and cook for 5 minutes.

3. Remove from the heat and reduce the pressure quickly under cold water. Test that the potatoes are really tender.

4. Drain the potatoes thoroughly and return them to the pan. Heat very gently for a few seconds, stirring to dry out. Remove from the heat.

5. Add the butter and milk and mash thoroughly with a potato masher, then beat with the masher or a wooden spoon until fluffy and smooth. Beat in the cheese until melted. Season with more salt, if necessary, and lots of pepper.

6. If you like, spoon the potato onto plates and make a small well in the top of each pile. Add a knob of butter and allow it to melt into a pool before serving.

I particularly like to use the tiny new potatoes for this; if you have larger ones, cut into even, bite-sized pieces before cooking to ensure they cook in the time. Always check and, if necessary, pressure cook a minute or so longer. For vegetarians, use a red pimento, cut into strips, instead of anchovies.

Serves 4–6 | Preparation time: 5 minutes | Cooking time: 6 minutes

Hot Potato Salad

700g baby new potatoes, scrubbed

300ml water

50g can of anchovies, drained

200ml crème fraîche

1 tsp lemon juice

A pinch of caster sugar

Freshly ground black pepper

To garnish

A sprinkling of sweet paprika

1. Put the potatoes in the pressure cooker with the water.

2. Cover with the lid and bring up to High pressure, then reduce the heat and cook for 4 minutes.

3. Remove from the heat and reduce the pressure quickly under cold water.

4. Drain the potatoes and return them to the pan.

5. Reserve 4 anchovies for garnish and finely chop the remainder. Mix with the crème fraîche, lemon juice, sugar and a little pepper. Add to the potatoes and toss lightly over a gentle heat.

6. Turn the potatoes into a warm serving dish. Cut the reserved anchovies in halves, lengthways. Arrange attractively on top, sprinkle with paprika and serve hot.

This is an unusual vegetable dish – the peppery watercress blends beautifully with the sweet carrots. It goes well with everything from fish to red meat and is really good with grilled chicken or, fro vegetarians, grilled Halloumi cheese.

Serves 4 | Preparation time: 5 minutes | Cooking time: 9 minutes | Vegetarian

Carrot and Watercress Braise

500g carrots, peeled and thickly sliced

250ml vegetable stock

Salt and freshly ground black pepper

2 handfuls of watercress leaves, chopped and thick stalks removed

1 tsp clear honey

A knob of butter

1. Put the carrots in the pressure cooker with the stock and a pinch of salt.

2. Cover with the lid and bring up to High pressure, then reduce the heat and cook for 3 minutes.

3. Remove from the heat and reduce the pressure quickly under cold water.

4. Return the cooker to the heat and bring to the boil, then boil rapidly until the liquid is reduced by half. Add the watercress leaves, honey and butter. Boil again for 2–3 minutes until the watercress is wilted and everything is bathed in a rich sauce. Stir gently taste and re-season, if necessary, before serving.

This is a delicious mixture of vegetables with a true taste of the Mediterranean. Serve it hot or cold, on its own; topped with grated cheese; fried or poached eggs; as an omelette or pancake filling; or as an accompaniment to grilled steaks, chops, chicken or fish.

Serves 4 | Preparation time: 15 minutes | Cooking time: 6 minutes | Vegetarian

Ratatouille

2 tbsp olive oil

1 red onion, sliced

1 aubergine, sliced

1 red pepper, sliced

1 green pepper, sliced

2 courgettes, sliced

1 garlic clove, crushed

2 beefsteak tomatoes, skinned and chopped

6 tbsp red wine

150ml passata

1 tsp caster sugar

Salt and freshly ground black pepper

1 tbsp chopped fresh thyme

1 tbsp chopped fresh basil

1 tbsp chopped fresh parsley

1. Heat the oil in the pressure cooker and fry the onion for 2 minutes, stirring. Add all the remaining ingredients except the basil and parsley and stir well.

2. Cover with the lid and bring up to High pressure, then reduce the heat and cook for 4 minutes.

3. Remove from the heat and reduce the pressure quickly under cold water.

4. Taste and re-season, if necessary, stir in the basil and parsley and serve.

Braised red cabbage is a classic, but using pears instead of apples makes it particularly good with gammon, venison, sausages or pork chops. Experiment and use white cabbage and white wine vinegar instead of red and, of course, apples instead of pears.

Serves 6 | Preparation time: 8 minutes | Cooking time: 6 minutes | Vegetarian

Spiced Braised Red Cabbage with Pears

1 small red cabbage, shredded

1 onion, thinly sliced

2 slightly unripe pears, peeled, cored and sliced

A large handful of raisins

Salt and freshly ground black pepper

2 tbsp soft light brown sugar

1 star anise

5cm piece of cinnamon stick

1 bay leaf

2 tbsp red wine vinegar

250ml water

1. Layer half the ingredients, except the bay leaf, spices, vinegar and water, in the pressure cooker. Repeat with a second layer. Add the water and vinegar. Tuck in the spice and bay leaf.

2. Cover with the lid and bring up to High pressure, then reduce the heat and cook for 4 minutes.

3. Remove from the heat and reduce the pressure quickly under cold water.

4. Return the open cooker to the heat and boil rapidly until the liquid has almost evaporated. Discard the spices and the bay leaf. Stir well, taste and re-season, if necessary. Serve hot.

Pumpkin seeds add a lovely nuttiness to this simple vegetable dish that's good with sausages, chops, black pudding, or even haggis. It also tastes good topped with fried eggs for a light lunch or supper.

Serves 4 | Preparation time: 7 minutes | Cooking time: 6 minutes | Vegetarian

Swede and Roasted Pumpkin Seed Champ

3 tbsp pumpkin seeds

1 small swede, diced

3 large, floury potatoes, diced

250ml vegetable stock

1 bunch of spring onions, chopped

Salt and freshly ground black pepper

4 tbsp dried milk powder

50g butter

1. Heat a non-stick frying pan. Add the pumpkin seeds and toss for a few minutes until lightly toasted. Tip out of the pan onto a plate immediately to prevent them from burning.

2. Put the swede and potatoes in the pressure cooker with the stock. Reserve a little of the chopped spring onions for garnish and put the remainder in the cooker. Season with salt and pepper.

3. Cover with the lid and bring up to High pressure, then reduce the heat and cook for 4 minutes.

4. Remove from the heat and reduce the pressure quickly under cold water.

5. Return the open cooker to the heat and boil to evaporate most of the liquid. Sprinkle in the milk powder and mash well. Taste and re-season, if necessary. Beat with a wooden spoon until fluffy, then beat in the pumpkin seeds.

6. Pile onto warm plates. Make a slight well in the centre of each pile of champ. Add a knob of butter to each and allow it to melt. Sprinkle with the chopped spring onion and serve.

This version of cauliflower cheese omits the necessity for making cheese sauce in a saucepan. It's for lazy cooks but it works really well so why not? Try it with broccoli too. It's also good with a handful of red cherry tomatoes added to the dish before grilling.

Serves 4 | Preparation time: 5 minutes | Cooking time: 8 minutes | Vegetarian

Creamy Cauliflower Cheese

1 small cauliflower, cut into large florets

300ml boiling water

Salt and freshly ground black pepper

150g strong Cheddar cheese, finely grated

150ml crème fraîche

½ tsp English mustard

To garnish

A handful of crushed cornflakes

1. Put the cauliflower in the pressure cooker with the water. Add a large pinch of salt.

2. Mix 100g of the cheese, the crème fraîche and mustard together in a small heatproof bowl. Add a little salt and pepper. Cover with foil, twisting and folding under the rim to secure. Place in the pressure cooker with the cauliflower.

3. Cover with the lid and bring up to High pressure, then reduce the heat and cook for 4 minutes.

4. Remove from the heat and reduce the pressure quickly under cold water.

5. Remove the sauce from the cooker and whisk until smooth.

6. Preheat the grill. Drain the cauliflower and transfer to a flameproof serving dish. Spoon the sauce over the cauliflower. Sprinkle with crushed cornflakes and remaining cheese and grill until golden and bubbling.

You can serve the simple cooked macedoine as a vegetable accompaniment to any meat or fish but this salad is delicious with cold meats or steamed oily fish like mackerel, herring or salmon. If you prefer a cold version, leave the vegetables to get completely cold before adding to the dressing.

Serves 4 | Preparation time: 10 minutes | Cooking time: 2 minutes | Vegetarian

Warm Russian Salad

For the macedoine

½ small swede, cut into small dice

1 large potato, cut into small dice

1 large carrot, peeled and cut into small dice

1 turnip, cut into small dice

300ml water

Salt and freshly ground black pepper

For the dressing

3 tbsp mayonnaise

3 tbsp crème fraîche

1 tbsp snipped fresh chives

1. Spread the vegetables out in the steamer basket in the pressure cooker. Place in the cooker with the water. Sprinkle with salt.

2. Cover with a lid and bring up to High pressure, then reduce the heat and cook for 2 minutes.

3. Remove from the heat and reduce the pressure quickly under cold water.

4. Drain the vegetables and return them to the pan. Add the mayonnaise and crème fraîche and season with a little salt and pepper. Toss well, then transfer to a serving dish. Sprinkle with the chives and serve while still warm.

A mild vegetable curry makes a great accompaniment to other meat, chicken or fish curries but can also be served as a dish in its own right – particularly with the addition of some protein in the form of diced paneer, fried eggs or some cooked chickpeas.

Serves 4 | Preparation time: 15 minutes | Cooking time: 6 minutes | Vegetarian

Mixed Vegetable Curry

25g butter

1 large onion, chopped

1 large garlic clove, crushed

2 tsp ground cumin

1 tsp ground turmeric

1 tbsp garam masala

250ml vegetable stock

2 tbsp tomato purée

½ tsp salt

1 tbsp lime juice

1 large carrot, peeled and sliced

1 aubergine, cut into small chunks

1 courgette, cut into chunky slices

1 red pepper, cut into small chunks

1 large potato, cut into small chunks

½ cauliflower, cut into florets

100g green beans, cut into short lengths

1 bay leaf

150g creamed coconut, chopped

1. Melt the butter in the pressure cooker. Add the onion and garlic and fry, stirring, for 2 minutes. Add the spices and fry for 30 seconds. Stir in the stock, tomato purée, salt and lime juice. Add all the vegetables and the bay leaf.

2. Cover with the lid and bring up to High pressure, then reduce the heat and cook for 4 minutes.

3. Remove from the heat and reduce the pressure quickly under cold water.

4. Scatter the pieces of coconut over, re-cover and seal and leave for a few minutes so the coconut softens and melts. Open the cooker and gently stir in over a low heat until the mixture thickens and bubbles. Taste and re-season, if necessary. Discard the bay leaf before serving.

This is a lovely combination that goes well with chicken, lamb or fish. You can make it with all peas instead of the mixture with broad beans, too. It can also be puréed and thinned with more stock or milk added for a delicious soup!

Serves 4 | Preparation time: 5 minutes (longer if shelling fresh pods) | Cooking time: 7 minutes | Vegetarian

Braised Peas with Lettuce and Broad Beans

50g butter

1 onion, finely chopped

175g fresh shelled or frozen peas

175g fresh shelled or frozen baby broad beans, skins removed, if liked

1 tbsp fresh chopped mint

1 little gem lettuce, shredded

250ml vegetable stock

Salt and freshly ground black pepper

1. Melt the butter in the pressure cooker. Add the onion and fry, stirring, for 2 minutes until softened but not browned. Add the remaining ingredients except the salt and pepper. Stir gently.

2. Cover with the lid and bring up to High pressure, then reduce the heat and cook for 2 minutes.

3. Remove from the heat and reduce the pressure quickly under cold water.

4. Open the cooker and boil rapidly for a few minutes to evaporate most of the liquid. Season to taste with salt and pepper and serve hot.

Serve this with any meat, chicken or fish curry as a moist accompaniment but it is also good as a curry in its own right. Alternatively, you can try it with some chunks of paneer or hard-boiled eggs stirred through it at the last moment.

Serves 4 | Preparation time: 3 minutes | Cooking time: 6 minutes | Vegetarian

Tarka Dhal

175g red lentils

1 large garlic clove, crushed

1 tbsp ground turmeric

1 tbsp ground cumin

1 tbsp ground coriander

2 tsp paprika

450ml vegetable stock

Salt and freshly ground black pepper

2 tbsp sunflower oil

1 onion, thinly sliced

1 tsp cumin seeds

1 tsp black mustard seeds

1. Put the lentils in the pressure cooker with the garlic, spices and stock. Add a little salt and pepper. Bring to the boil, then reduce the heat to medium.

2. Cover with the lid and bring up to High pressure over a medium heat, then remove from the heat and allow the pressure to reduce slowly at room temperature.

3. Meanwhile, heat the oil in a frying pan and fry the onion for 5 minutes until golden, stirring all the time. Stir in the seeds and fry a further minute until they start to pop.

4. Open the pressure cooker. Taste and re-season the lentils. Stir in the onion and spice seed mixture and serve hot.

Chapter 15

Desserts

Steamed puddings are light and luscious – and no fuggy kitchen to contend with. Rice is sweet, tender and creamy, custards set quickly and simply, and fruit can be poached or stewed to perfection. Your pressure cooker can create a whole array of delicious desserts from everyday puds to dinner party masterpieces and, like all other dishes, it does it in record time. Make sure you adhere the pre-steaming without pressure for sponge and suet puds to allow them to rise or you'll end up with a heavy, solid mass. Also ensure you use the right level of pressure – it is important for perfect results. All these recipes are suitable for vegetarians.

This is a firm family favourite – it cheats using chocolate spread for the lovely gooey topping instead of fiddling with various ingredients. It goes down a treat with either vanilla ice cream, clotted cream, thick pouring cream or, for chocoholics, chocolate-flavoured custard!

Serves 4–6 | Preparation time: 10 minutes | Cooking time: 35 minutes, plus pressure reducing time

Melting Chocolate Pudding

A knob of butter

3 tbsp dark chocolate spread

2 tbsp hot water

100g softened butter

100g caster sugar

75g self-raising flour

25g cocoa powder

1 tsp baking powder

2 eggs

2 tbsp milk

2 tbsp lemon juice

1. Grease a 1 litre pudding basin. Mix together the chocolate spread and hot water until blended and spoon into the base of the basin.

2. Put all the remaining ingredients except the lemon juice in a bowl and beat with an electric whisk or wooden spoon until smooth. Transfer the mixture to the prepared basin, making sure the sauce is completely covered. Level the surface. Cover with a double thickness of baking parchment with a pleat in the middle. Twist and fold under the rim to secure or tie with string.

3. Place 1 litre boiling water in the pressure cooker and add the lemon juice to the water (to prevent pan staining). Either add the trivet and stand the basin on it, or put the basin in the steamer basket and place in the water.

4. Cover with the lid but do not seal. Cook over a low heat without pressure, allowing steam to escape, for 15 minutes. Then seal the cooker and bring up to Low pressure, then reduce the heat and cook for 25 minutes.

5. Remove from the heat and allow the pressure to reduce slowly at room temperature.

6. Remove the pudding from the cooker, remove the paper, loosen the edge and turn out onto a serving plate. Serve hot.

You can use ordinary golden syrup for this but the maple syrup – although expensive – adds a fabulous flavour! You can omit the pecans or use walnuts instead if you prefer as well. Another variation is to use slightly unripe pears instead of apples.

Serves 6 | Preparation time: 10 minutes | Cooking time: 40 minutes

Steamed Apple, Pecan and Maple Syrup Sponge Pudding

100g self-raising flour

1 tsp baking powder

100g soft light brown sugar

100g softened butter, plus a little extra for greasing

1 tsp ground cinnamon

50g pecans, roughly chopped

2 eggs

2 tbsp milk

3 tbsp maple syrup

2 large cooking apples, peeled, cored and thinly sliced

1 tbsp lemon juice

To serve

Cream

1. Put the flour, sugar, softened butter, cinnamon, nuts, eggs and milk in a bowl and beat with a wooden spoon or electric beater until fluffy and blended.

2. Lightly grease a 1.5 litre pudding basin and line the base and a little way up the sides with baking parchment. Put the syrup in the dish, then add the apples. Cover with the sponge mixture and level the surface. Cover the dish with a double thickness of baking parchment with large pleat in the centre to allow for rising. Twist and fold the parchment under the rim to secure or tie with string.

3. Add 1 litre boiling water to the cooker with the lemon juice. Stand the bowl on the trivet in the cooker or put it in the steamer basket and place in the water.

4. Cover with the lid but do not seal. Cook over a low heat without pressure, allowing steam to escape, for 15 minutes. Then seal the cooker and bring up to Low pressure, then reduce the heat and cook for 25 minutes.

5. Remove from the heat and allow the pressure to reduce slowly at room temperature.

6. Remove the foil, loosen the edge, turn the pudding out onto a serving dish and remove the paper. Serve with cream.

Another classic that just couldn't be overlooked. It's the nursery pud to top all nursery puds! Cooking it in the pressure cooker renders it light and luscious in record time. I always use vegetable suet but use beef suet if you prefer. Stoned raisins give maximum flavour, though seedless can be used instead.

Serves 6 | Preparation time: 7 minutes | Cooking time: 1 hour

Spotted Dick

100g self-raising lour

50g fresh white breadcrumbs

75g shredded vegetable suet

3 tbsp caster sugar

75g stoned raisins

50g sultanas

50g currants

Cold water to mix

1 tbsp lemon juice

To serve

Warmed golden syrup

Custard

1. Grease a 1.2 litre pudding basin and line the base with a circle of baking parchment.

2. Mix the flour with the breadcrumbs, suet and sugar, then stir in the fruit. Mix with enough water to form a soft but not sticky dough and put in the basin. Cover with a double thickness of baking parchment with a pleat in the middle to allow for rising. Tie it securely with string or twist and fold under the rim to secure (it's vital no water gets in under the paper).

3. Add 1 litre boiling water to the pressure cooker with the lemon juice. Place the pudding on the trivet or in the steaming basket without the trivet in the pressure cooker.

4. Cover with the lid but do not seal. Cook over a low heat without pressure, allowing steam to escape, for 15 minutes. Then seal the cooker and bring up to Low pressure, then reduce the heat and cook for 45 minutes.

5. Remove from the heat and allow the pressure to reduce slowly at room temperature.

6. Remove the paper, loosen the edge then turn out onto a serving plate. Serve with warm syrup and custard.

You can't beat a good, creamy rice pudding but it takes hours slow-cooking it in the oven. Here it's very quick and, for those of you who like skin, the recipe tells you how to decant it and brown it off at the end if you like.

Serves 4 | Preparation time: 5 minutes | Cooking time: 14 minutes, plus browning (optional)

Vanilla Rice Pudding

A knob of butter

410g can of evaporated milk

75g short-grain rice

50g caster sugar

1 vanilla pod

1. Melt the butter in the pressure cooker. Add the evaporated milk. Fill the can with water and add that too. Bring the milk to the boil in the open cooker, taking care that it doesn't boil over. Add the rice and sugar. Split the vanilla pod lengthways, scrape the seeds into the pan, then add the pod. Stir and bring the milk back to the boil. As it is beginning to rise up again, turn down the heat to medium so it is gently simmering.

2. Cover with the lid and bring up to High pressure over a medium heat, then reduce the heat and cook for 12 minutes.

3. Remove from the heat and allow the pressure to reduce slowly at room temperature.

4. Stir well and discard the vanilla pod.

5. If you like a skin on the top, preheat the grill. Spoon the pudding into a flameproof serving dish and pop under the grill until the top is golden brown.

The perfect refreshing fruit dish to serve hot with custard and, perhaps, some crunchy shortbread, or cold with vanilla ice cream and, maybe, some gorgeous gooey-in-the-centre meringues. It's good with plain yoghurt for breakfast too.

Serves 4 | Preparation time: 5 minutes | Cooking time: 3–5 minutes

Rhubarb and Fresh Ginger Compôte

450g rhubarb, trimmed and cut into short lengths

4 tbsp water

75g caster sugar

2.5cm piece fresh root ginger, peeled and cut into wafer thin slices

1. Put the rhubarb in a soufflé dish that will fit in the cooker. Add the water, sugar and ginger slices to the dish. Put the trivet in the pressure cooker and add about 300ml water to the pan. Put the dish of rhubarb on the trivet.

2. Cover with the lid and bring up to High pressure, then reduce the heat and cook for 3 minutes for forced rhubarb, 5 minutes for thicker outdoor sticks.

3. Remove from the heat and allow the pressure to reduce slowly at room temperature.

4. Taste and add more sugar if necessary. Serve warm or cold.

This takes a fraction of the time it takes to cook in the oven and is always soft and creamy. It's worth crisping it up under the grill for a lovely, sweet, crunchy top but watch it as it can burn easily.

Serves 4 | Preparation time: 10 minutes | Cooking time: 8 minutes

Bread and Butter Pudding

4 slices of buttered bread, cut into 4 triangles

2 handfuls of mixed dried fruit

2 large eggs

2 tbsp caster sugar

450ml milk

1 tsp natural vanilla extract

Freshly grated nutmeg

1 tbsp lemon juice

2 tbsp soft light brown sugar

1. Butter an 18cm flameproof soufflé dish and layer the bread and dried fruit in it. Whisk together the eggs, sugar, milk and vanilla and pour over the bread. Grate plenty of nutmeg over the top. Cover with a double thickness of baking parchment, twisting and folding under the rim to secure, or tie it with string.

2. Place 1 litre water in the cooker and add the lemon juice. Place the dish on the trivet, or in the steamer basket, without the trivet in the pressure cooker.

3. Cover with the lid and bring up to High pressure, then reduce the heat and cook for 5 minutes.

4. Remove from the heat and allow the pressure to reduce slowly at room temperature.

5. Preheat the grill. Remove the pudding from the cooker and take off the paper. Sprinkle with the demerara sugar. Place the dish in the grill pan and grill until the top is lightly toasted.

Always use firm pears for this recipe. If they are overripe, they'll 'fall' as you cook them. You can cook apples or quinces in the same way. If you are cooking quinces, you'll need to increase the sugar quantity to about 120g.

Serves 4 | Preparation time: 5 minutes | Cooking time: 6 minutes

Spiced Pears in Red Wine

400ml red wine

90g caster sugar

4 firm pears, peeled but left whole

2 cloves

1 piece of cinnamon stick

1 star anise

To serve

Cream

1. Put the wine and sugar in the pressure cooker and stir over a gentle heat until dissolved. Place the pears in the wine and turn over to coat completely. Tuck the spices around.

2. Cover with the lid and bring up to Low pressure, then reduce the heat and cook for 6 minutes.

3. Remove from the heat and allow the pressure to reduce slowly at room temperature.

4. Open the cooker and turn the pears over occasionally as they cool so they colour evenly. Leave until warm or cool, then chill. Discard the spices before serving warm or cold with cream.

I've done a coffee-flavoured crème caramel to be a little bit different, but to make plain ones, simply omit the coffee flavouring. Timing is crucial as the custard will curdle if overcooked.

Serves 4 | Preparation time: 10 minutes | Cooking time: 3 minutes, plus chilling

Coffee Crème Caramel

3 tbsp granulated sugar

3 tbsp water

2 large eggs

2 tbsp caster sugar

150ml single cream

200ml milk

½ tsp natural vanilla extract

1 tsp instant coffee

1 tsp water

1 tbsp lemon juice

1. Warm four dariole moulds or ramekins. Put the granulated sugar and water in a small saucepan. Heat, stirring until the sugar dissolves, without boiling. Then bring to the boil and boil until a rich golden brown without stirring. Pour into the dariole moulds or ramekins. Using a cloth to protect hands from the hot caramel, quickly swirl the pots so the caramel coats the base and a little way up the sides.

2. Whisk the eggs, sugar, cream, milk and vanilla together. Dissolve the coffee in the water and whisk in. Strain into the moulds. Stand them in the steaming basket and place on the trivet in the cooker containing 750ml boiling water and the lemon juice (if necessary, balance one of the moulds on top of the other three). Lay a sheet of baking parchment over the moulds.

3. Cover with the lid and bring up to High pressure, then reduce the heat and cook for 3 minutes only.

4. Remove from the heat and allow the pressure to reduce slowly at room temperature. Remove from the cooker, leave to cool, then chill.

5. When ready to serve, loosen the edges and turn out onto serving dishes.

There's nothing like homemade Christmas pudding. It is so simple to make, and getting everyone to stir the mixture and make a wish is a lovely tradition worth preserving. Unlike having to boil it for hours and hours to get it really dark – steaming up the kitchen and with the threat of it boiling dry – it's easy in the pressure cooker, you just leave it to do its stuff. This is best made a month or two before Christmas to allow the flavours to develop.

Makes 1 large pudding | Preparation time: 15 minutes | Cooking time: 3 hours, plus 30 minutes to reheat

Christmas Pudding with Guinness, Apple and Brandy

500g mixed dried fruit

3 tbsp brandy

2 eating apples, grated

1 large carrot, peeled and grated

100g shredded vegetable suet

75g soft dark brown sugar

175g fresh white breadcrumbs

1 large egg, beaten

50g plain flour

1½ tsp mixed spice

¼ tsp freshly grated nutmeg

½ tsp ground cinnamon

150ml Guinness or other stout

1 tbsp lemon juice

A little caster sugar and a sprig of holly, to decorate

1. Mix the fruit, brandy or cognac and leave to soak for 2–3 hours.

2. Mix in all the remaining ingredients except the lemon juice. At this point let the members of the family have a stir and make a wish! If you have time, cover the bowl and leave to stand for 24 hours.

3. Grease a 1.2 litre pudding basin and line the base with a circle of baking parchment.

4. Spoon the pudding mixture into the basin and press down well. Cover with a circle of baking parchment then a saucer that will fit neatly on top (or use double-thickness parchment). Cover the basin with a double thickness of foil, twisting and folding under the rim to secure. Stand the basin on the trivet, or in the steaming basket, in the pressure cooker with 2 litres of boiling water and the lemon juice. Cover without sealing and steam for 15 minutes.

5. Bring up to High pressure, then reduce the heat and cook for 3 hours.

6. Remove from the heat and allow the pressure to reduce slowly at room temperature. The pudding should be good and dark.

7. Leave to cool, then re-wrap in clean foil and store in a cool, dark place.

For the brandy butter

100g unsalted butter, at room temperature

100g soft dark brown sugar or sifted icing sugar

6 tbsp brandy

To serve

A little caster sugar

5 tbsp brandy, (optional)

Whipped or pouring cream

A sprig of holly

To make the brandy butter

1. Put the butter and sugar in a food processor and blend until smooth, then gradually mx in the brandy, a little at a time, until well blended. Alternatively, you can use a hand whisk. Pack into a small bowl, cover and keep in the fridge for a few days or in the freezer if you are making it in advance.

On Christmas Day

1. On the day, once again, stand the basin on the trivet or in the steaming basket in the pressure cooker with 2 litres of boiling water and the lemon juice.

2. Cover with the lid and bring up to High pressure over a medium heat, then reduce the heat and cook for 30 minutes.

3. Remove from the heat and allow the pressure to reduce slowly at room temperature.

4. Turn the pudding out, dust with caster sugar and press the holly sprig in the top.

5. If using the brandy, warm it in a ladle or small pan. Ignite it and quickly pour over the pudding and take it to the table flaming.

6. Serve with the brandy butter and cream.

This is an old-fashioned pudding that tastes so good, it's due for a revival! The apples will keep hot in the pan, once pressure is reduced, whilst you enjoy the main course. They're also good with scoops of vanilla or ginger ice cream.

Serves 4 | Preparation time: 10 minutes | Cooking time: 3–4 minutes

Stuffed Apples

A litle butter

4 even-sized cooking apples that will fit in the pressure cooker, washed and cored

50g light brown sugar

1/2 tsp mixed spice

50g walnuts, chopped

1 tbsp lemon juice

50g sultanas

4 tsp golden syrup

To serve

Clotted cream or custard

1. Line the steaming basket with foil. Score a line round the middle of each apple to prevent the skins splitting when pressure-cooked. Stand them in the foil-lined steaming basket. Mix together all the remaining ingredients except the golden syrup. Pack into the holes where the cores had been.

2. Add 250ml water to the pressure cooker and add the lemon juice, then put the basket of apples on the trivet in the cooker. Wet a teaspoon, then spoon the syrup over each apple.

3. Cover with the lid and bring up to High pressure, then reduce the heat and cook for 3 minutes.

4. Remove from the heat and allow the pressure to reduce slowly at room temperature.

5. Test the apples, and if they are not completely soft, bring back to High pressure and cook for another minute, then allow the pressure to reduce slowly again.

6. Carefully transfer the apples to serving dishes and serve hot with cream or custard.

This is a rich and delicious dessert-cum-cake. I like to fill the centre with whipped cream and serve it with coffee, but you could pile it full of raspberries, or even blueberries if you prefer, and serve with pouring cream.

Serves 6–8 | Preparation time: 10 minutes | Cooking time: 20 minutes

Chocolate Truffle Ring

Sunflower oil for greasing

225g plain, good-quality chocolate

60g self-raising flour

40g cocoa

1 tsp baking powder

100g butter, softened

100g caster sugar

2 eggs, separated

2 tsp natural vanilla extract

150g fine fresh white bread or cake crumbs

175ml milk

1 tbsp lemon juice

1. Oil a 20cm ring mould (preferably fluted).

2. Break up 100g of the chocolate and melt in a bowl over a pan of gently simmering water.

3. Sift the flour, cocoa and baking powder together.

4. Beat the butter and sugar together in a bowl until light and fluffy. Beat in the melted chocolate, egg yolk and vanilla. Add half the crumbs, half the flour and half the milk. Fold in gently with a metal spoon. Add the remaining halves and fold in again.

5. Whisk the egg whites until stiff, then fold in with a metal spoon.

6. Turn into the prepared mould and level the surface. Cover with oiled foil. Twist and fold all round to secure. Place the trivet in the pressure cooker and pour in 750ml boiling water and the lemon juice. Place the mould on the trivet. Cover with the lid but do not seal, and steam without pressure for 10 minutes.

7. Seal and bring up to Low pressure, then reduce the heat and cook for 10 minutes.

8. Remove from the heat and allow the pressure to reduce slowly at room temperature.

9. Remove from the cooker and leave to cool for 5 minutes.

10. Turn out the cake onto a wire rack to cool.

11. Transfer to a serving plate. Melt the remaining chocolate as before and spoon all over the top, allowing it to trickle down the sides. Leave to set.

Chapter 16

Breads and Cakes

Bread and cakes are not things you would immediately associate with pressure cooking and, of course, they won't have the brown crusty element of recipes baked in the oven, but they do have a wonderful light, moist quality that makes them utterly delicious.

Some of the cakes are covered in frosting or other coatings so the lack of a brown crust is disguised (a bit like you'd do with microwaved ones) but many have a rich, dark colour anyway, so it isn't a problem. Like steamed puddings, you do need to steam without pressure first to allow for rising. If you omit this, you will get very disappointing, heavy results so don't try and cut corners! All these recipes are suitable for vegetarians.

This steamed milk bread is traditionally cooked in a pudding cloth, then cut with a wire or strong thread into slices. If you use a knife, you would squash it. You could experiment with a cheese wire if you have one or just gently pull it into pieces if you don't want to do the 'thread treatment' below.

Makes 1 loaf | Preparation time: 5 minutes, plus rising | Cooking time: 30 minutes

Czech Knedlíky

250ml milk

300g plain flour

1 tsp fast-action dried yeast

$1/4$ tsp salt

$1/2$ tsp caster sugar

1 egg

1 tbsp lemon juice

1. Heat the milk to hand-hot. Tip into a food processor with the dough hook. Add all the remaining ingredients except the lemon juice and run the machine until you have a smooth dough. Continue to run the machine for 1 minute to knead the dough. Alternatively, put the milk in a bowl, add the remaining ingredients and mix with a knife until beginning to form a dough, then draw together with the hands to form a ball. Turn out onto a lightly floured surface and knead for about 5 minutes until smooth and elastic.

2. Lay out a large sheet of foil and place a sheet of baking parchment on top.

3. Roll the dough into a thick sausage that will fit in the pressure cooker and place on the parchment. Wrap loosely, sealing the top and ends well, allowing room for the dough to rise. Wrap loosely in a second sheet of foil, repeating the process to make sure that water cannot get in. Place in the steaming basket and leave in a warm place for 45 minutes to rise.

4. Place 1 litre boiling water in the pressure cooker with the lemon juice. Add the trivet, then put the steaming basket on top. Cover with the lid but do not seal, then steam without pressure for 10 minutes.

5. Seal and bring up to Low pressure over a medium heat, then reduce the heat and cook for 20 minutes.

6. Remove from the heat and allow the pressure to reduce slowly at room temperature.

7. Cool slightly, then unwrap and tip onto a board with a piece of sewing thread laid across it towards one end. Lift either end of the thread up and cross it over the top of the bread and pull to cut a slice. Move the thread along and slice again.

This soft, spongy loaf has delicious almost brioche-like taste and texture and is delicious served with any soup or main course to mop up luscious juices, but is also good, pulled apart and spread with butter and jam or marmalade, or when a day old, sliced and toasted.

Makes 1 round loaf | Preparation time: 10 minutes, plus rising | Cooking time: 30 minutes

Steamed Seeded Loaf

275g strong white flour, plus extra for dusting

1 sachet fast-action dried yeast

2 tsp caster sugar

1 tsp salt

1 tbsp sunflower oil

175ml hand-hot water

15g butter, melted

1 tsp caraway or poppy seeds

1 tbsp lemon juice

1. Mix the flour with the yeast, sugar and salt in a bowl. Add the oil, then stir in enough water to form a soft but not sticky, dough. Knead gently on a lightly floured surface for 5 minutes until smooth and elastic. Alternatively, blend all the ingredients in a food processor and run the machine for 1 minute to knead.

2. Put the dough in a greased polythene bag and leave in a warm place to rise for 1 hour.

3. Re-knead the dough briefly then shape into a round. Line the steaming basket with oiled foil then baking parchment. Place the bread round in the basket.

4. Mix the butter with the caraway seeds and gently brush all over the top of the bread.

5. Place the trivet in the pressure cooker and pour in 500ml boiling water and the lemon juice. Cover the pressure cooker with the lid and leave the dough to rise for 30 minutes until well risen again. Cover with the lid but do not seal, and steam for 10 minutes.

6. Seal and bring up to Low pressure, then reduce the heat and cook for 20 minutes.

7. Remove from the heat and allow the pressure to reduce slowly at room temperature.

8. Carefully remove the lid, lift out the bread and leave to cool slightly. Serve torn into pieces or cut into wedges.

This traditional English afternoon tea classic is equally good for dessert, topped with raspberries and served with cream. The easiest way to coat it when cooked is to glaze the sizes and roll in coconut before glazing and dusting the top. If you coat the top first, the sides are very tricky!

Makes an 18cm cake | Preparation time: 10 minutes | Cooking time: 40 minutes

Vanilla Coconut Sponge

150g softened butter

150g caster sugar

150g self-raising flour

1 tsp baking powder

2 large eggs, beaten

1 tsp natural vanilla extract

2 tbsp milk

1 tbsp lemon juice

3 tbsp seedless raspberry jam, warmed

3–4 tbsp desiccated coconut

A few glacé cherries, halved (optional)

1. Grease an 18cm soufflé dish and line the base with a circle of baking parchment.

2. Put the butter, sugar, flour, baking powder and eggs in a bowl and beat with a wooden spoon or electric whisk until smooth and fluffy. Beat in the milk to make a soft dropping consistency. Spoon into the prepared dish. Cover with a double thickness baking parchment, twisting and folding under the rim to secure.

3. Put the trivet or steaming basket in the pressure cooker and pour in 500ml boiling water and the lemon juice. Add the dish. Cover with the lid but do not seal, and steam for 15 minutes over a low heat.

4. Bring up to Low pressure, then reduce the heat and cook for 25 minutes.

5. Remove from the heat and allow the pressure to reduce slowly at room temperature.

6. Remove from the cooker and leave to cool for 10 minutes then turn out onto a wire rack.

7. When cold, brush the sides with warmed jam. Put the coconut on a plate and gently roll the cake in it to coat. Then brush the top and dust with the remaining coconut. Top with a few halved glacé cherries, if using, and leave to set.

This is best made a few days before eating, then stored in an airtight tin. It becomes much stickier as it matures slightly. Try slices topped with mashed bananas and a dollop of cream for an impromptu dessert too. For a lighter loaf, use golden syrup instead of treacle.

Makes 1 loaf | Preparation time: 7 minutes | Cooking time: 40 minutes

Gingerbread Loaf

100g wholemeal flour

50g plain flour

½ tsp salt

½ tsp ground cinnamon

2 tsp ground ginger

1 tsp bicarbonate of soda

3 tbsp black treacle

75g soft dark brown sugar

25g butter, plus extra for spreading

250ml milk

1 tbsp lemon juice

To serve

A little butter

1. Grease a 450g loaf tin and line with baking parchment.

2. Mix the flours, salt, cinnamon, ginger and bicarbonate of soda thoroughly together in a large bowl.

3. Warm the treacle, sugar and butter in a saucepan until the fat melts. Stir in the milk.

4. Pour a little at a time into the flour mixture and mix thoroughly until smooth.

5. Turn into the prepared tin. Cover with a double thickness of baking parchment, with a pleat in the middle to allow for rising. Twist and fold under the rim to secure or tie with string. Put the trivet or the steamer basket in the pressure cooker. Pour 750ml boiling water and the lemon juice into the cooker. Add the loaf. Cover with the lid but do not seal, and boil without pressure for 15 minutes to allow for expansion.

6. Seal and bring up to Low pressure, then reduce the heat and steam for 25 minutes.

7. Remove from the heat and allow the pressure to reduce slowly at room temperature.

8. Remove the loaf from the cooker and leave to cool slightly. Turn out, remove the paper and leave to cool on a wire rack.

9. Serve sliced and buttered.

If you are a nut fan, replace 50g mixed dried cake fruit with chopped mixed nuts. You could use all cherries or chopped dried apricots and raisins instead of the mixed fruit for a change. The dark brown sugar gives the best colour but you can use light brown if you prefer.

Makes an 18cm cake | Preparation time: 10 minutes | Cooking time: 1hour 5 minutes

Steamed Fruit Cake

100g butter, softened

100g soft dark brown sugar

2 eggs

2 tbsp milk

275g plain flour

2 tsp baking powder

1 tsp mixed spice

1 tsp ground cinnamon

350g mixed dried cake fruit

1 tbsp demerara sugar

1 tbsp lemon juice

1. Grease an 18cm, deep, round soufflé dish and line the base with baking parchment.

2. Put all the ingredients except the fruit, demerara sugar and lemon juice in a large mixing bowl and beat with a wooden spoon or an electric whisk until smooth and well blended. Fold in the fruit.

3. Spoon the mixture into the prepared dish and level the surface. Cover with a double thickness of baking parchment with a pleat in the middle to allow for expansion. Twist and fold under the rim to secure, or tie with string. Place the trivet or the steamer basket in the pressure cooker. Add 750ml boiling water and the lemon juice. Add the soufle dish. Cover with the lid but do not seal, then boil without pressure for 15 minutes to allow for expansion.

4. Seal and bring up to Low pressure, then reduce the heat and steam for 50 minutes.

5. Remove from the heat and allow the pressure to reduce slowly at room temperature.

6. Lift the cake out of the cooker, remove the foil and sprinkle liberally with the demerara sugar. Leave to cool for 15 minutes.

7. Loosen the edge, remove from the dish, discard the cooking paper and leave to cool on a wire rack.

This is delicious served sliced and buttered, or try it spread with soft white cheese and some thinly sliced fresh pears for a decadent treat. You can omit the walnuts if you prefer. It's good toasted when a day or two old, too.

Makes a 450g loaf | Preparation time: 10 minutes | Cooking time: 45 minutes

Raisin and Walnut Tea Bread

225g self-raising flour

1/2 tsp baking powder

1/4 tsp salt

1/2 tsp mixed spice

75g butter, cut into pieces

50g soft light brown sugar

100g raisins

50g walnuts, chopped

1 large egg

2 tbsp milk

1 tbsp lemon juice

To serve

Butter

1. Grease a 450g loaf tin and line with baking parchment.

2. Sift the flour, baking powder, salt and spice together. Add the butter and rub in with the fingertips until the mixture resembles breadcrumbs. Stir in all the remaining ingredients except the lemon juice, adding enough milk to form a firm dough.

3. Turn the mixture into the prepared tin and level the surface. Cover with a double thickness of baking parchment with a pleat in the middle, twisting and folding under the rim to secure or tied with string. Place the trivet or the steamer basket in the pressure cooker. Add 750ml boiling water and the lemon juice. Add the loaf tin. Cover with the lid but do not seal, then boil without pressure for 15 minutes to allow for expansion.

4. Seal and bring up to Low pressure, then reduce the heat and steam for 30 minutes.

5. Remove from the heat and allow the pressure to reduce slowly at room temperature.

6. Preheat the grill. Carefully remove the paper and place the tin under the grill to lightly brown the top.

7. Leave to cool for 10 minutes, then turn out onto a wire rack, remove the paper and leave to cool completely.

8. Serve sliced and buttered.

Chapter 17

Preserves

A pressure cooker makes a great preserving pan and speeds up proceedings incredibly. The cooker is used to soften the fruit for marmalade, jam or chutney but it still needs boiling in the open cooker to reach setting point or a thick consistency. Remember, if adapting your own recipes, the proportion of sugar and fruit remains the same but you must cut the water by half as very little will be lost to evaporation during the softening period under pressure. Because soft fruit, like strawberries or raspberries, don't need pre-cooking, I haven't included recipes for making them into jam here. All these recipes are suitable for vegetarians.

To test for a set

Remove the preserve from the heat. Lift up a wooden spoonful of the preserve, turn it above the pan twice so the preserve drops off it, then hold the spoon and watch the last drop. If it stays as a jelly-like blob hanging off the spoon, setting point is reached.

Alternatively, put a small spoonful on a cold saucer. Leave to stand for a minute, then run a finger through it. If the preserve wrinkles and leaves a clear line, setting point has been reached.

Seville oranges are only in for a short period of time in January/February but do use them in exactly the same way when they are in season. You'll need 1kg of Seville oranges instead of the three fruits. If you don't like shreds in the marmalade, simply don't shred the cooked shells; discard them and make jelly marmalade instead.

Makes about 2.5kg (6 jars) | Preparation time: 25 minutes | Cooking time: 12 minutes

Three-fruit Marmalade

1 grapefruit

2 large oranges

1 lemon

750ml water

1.7kg preserving sugar

1. Scrub the fruit under cold water. Cut the fruit in halves, squeeze out the juice, reserving the pips. Strain the juice into the pressure cooker. Scrape out the pulp and membranes from the fruit rind using a serrated-edged grapefruit knife. Add the shells to the cooker and pour in the water.

2. Tip the pith, pips, membranes and any bits into a piece of muslin or a new disposable kitchen cloth. Tie up securely and add to the cooker.

3. Cover with the lid and bring up to High pressure, then reduce the heat and cook for 10 minutes.

4. Remove from the heat and allow the pressure to reduce slowly at room temperature.

5. Carefully lift out the bag of pulp and pips and squeeze against the side of the pan with the back of the spoon to extract all the juice. Lift out the fruit shells and leave until cool enough to handle, then cut into shreds – as thickly or thinly as you like.

6. Return the shreds to the cooker and add the squeezed lemon juice and sugar. Heat gently, stirring until the sugar has dissolved.

7. Bring to the boil in the open cooker, and boil rapidly until setting point is reached (see page 179). It will happen very quickly.

8. Pot in clean, warm jars, cool, label and store in a cool, dark place. Once opened, store in the fridge and use within a few weeks.

You don't have to add the brandy but I love the luxurious flavour it adds. Simply increase the water by the same amount if you prefer. Boozy alternatives would be amaretto, liqueur or port.

Makes about 1.5kg (4 jars) | Preparation time: 10 minutes | Cooking time: 15 minutes

Plum Brandy Jam

1kg plums

250ml water

50ml brandy

1kg preserving sugar

1. Wash, halve and stone the fruit. Tie the stones loosely in a muslin bag or new disposable kitchen cloth. Place the fruit and the bag of stones in the pressure cooker with the water.

2. Cover with the lid and bring up to High pressure, then reduce the heat and cook for 10 minutes.

3. Remove from the heat and allow the pressure to reduce at room temperature.

4. Open the cooker, lift out the bag of stones with a spoon, pressing it firmly against the side of the pan to extract maximum juice. Mash the fruit down into the juice with a wooden spoon or potato peeler.

5. Add the brandy and sugar. Stir over a gentle heat in the open cooker until the sugar has completely dissolved.

6. Bring to the boil and boil rapidly until setting point is reached (see page 179).

7. Pot in clean, warm jars, cool, label and store in a cool, dark place. Once opened, store in the fridge and use within a few weeks.

The nuts and amaretti add a delicious contrast and flavour to this simple jam, but they can be omitted if preferred. It is particularly good served with warm brioche or croissants for breakfast.

Makes about 2 kg (4–5 jars) | Preparation time: 5 minutes | Cooking time: 8–13 minutes

Dried Apricot and Almond Jam

450g ready-to eat dried apricots

1 litre water

2 tbsp lemon juice

1.4kg preserving sugar

50g blanched almonds

2 tbsp amaretto liqueur (optional)

1. Snip the apricots into quarters with wet scissors and place in the pressure cooker. Add the water and lemon juice.

2. Cover with the lid and bring up to High pressure, then cook for 3 minutes.

3. Remove from the heat and allow the pressure to reduce slowly at room temperature.

4. Stir in the sugar, almonds and liqueur, if using, and dissolve over a low heat, stirring continuously. Bring to the boil and boil rapidly for 5–10 minutes until setting point is reached (see page 179).

5. Leave to cool slightly so the nuts don't rise to the surface of the potted jam, then pot in clean, warm jars. Cool, label and store in a cool dark place. Once opened, store in the fridge and eat within a few weeks.

I like to use cooking apples for this but you could use tart eating ones if you prefer. I also like the more intensive flavour you get by using apple juice instead of water but the choice is yours.

Makes about 1.75 kg (5 jars) | Preparation time: 20 minutes | Cooking time: 10 minutes

Blackberry and Apple Jam

1kg blackberries

350g cooking apples

1 tbsp lemon juice

150ml apple juice or water

1.35kg preserving sugar

1. Pick over and hull the blackberries, then wash them. Place in the pressure cooker. Peel, core and chop the apples and add them to the blackberries. Put the peel, core and pips in a muslin bag or tie in a new disposable kitchen cloth. Add to the pressure cooker with the lemon juice and apple juice or water.

2. Cover with the lid and bring up to High pressure, then reduce the heat and cook for 6 minutes.

3. Remove from the heat and allow the pressure to reduce slowly at room temperature.

4. Remove the bag of peel and pips and squeeze against the side of the pan with a wooden spoon, to extract all the juice. Mash the fruit well down in the juice.

5. Stir in the sugar in the open cooker over a gentle heat until completely dissolved.

6. Bring to the boil and boil rapidly until a set is reached (see page 179).

7. Pot in clean, warm jars, cool, label and store in a cool, dark place. Once opened, store in the fridge and use within a few weeks.

This is my favourite combination and great to serve with roast lamb, in particular. It is also good with chicken, game birds and pork. You can use water instead of cider or make apple and mint jelly by simply substituting chopped mint for the rosemary. Alternatively, you can omit the added flavouring altogether if you prefer.

Makes about 1.25kg (4 small jars) | Preparation time: 15 minutes, plus straining | Cooking time: 8 minutes

Apple, Cider and Rosemary Jelly

500g cooking apples

1 lemon, scrubbed and chopped

500ml cider

Granulated sugar

20g fresh rosemary leaves, finely chopped

1. Wash the apples, cut out any bruises and chop roughly. Place in the pressure cooker with the lemon and cider. Bring to the boil in the open cooker and press down well with a wooden spoon or potato masher.

2. Cover the pan, bring up to High pressure, then reduce the heat and cook for 5 minutes.

3. Remove from the heat and allow the pressure to reduce slowly at room temperature.

4. Mash the fruit to a pulp in the liquid. Strain through a jelly bag or through a sieve lined with a new disposable kitchen cloth, suspended over a bowl. Don't squeeze the bag or press the fruit or the result will be cloudy.

5. Measure the liquid and calculate the amount of sugar needed – you should use 400g sugar to 500ml liquid. Rinse out the cooker.

6. Return the juice to the pressure cooker and add the correct amount of sugar and the rosemary. Heat gently in the open pan until the sugar dissolves, stirring occasionally.

7. Bring to the boil and boil briefly until setting point is reached (see page 179). It will only take a couple of minutes. Skim the surface very quickly, if necessary.

8. Pot in clean, warm jars, cool, label and store in a cool dark place. Once opened, store in the fridge and use within three weeks.

You can make all lemon curd by substituting the limes with a large lemon but I love the fragrance you get with the combination of the two. It doesn't keep as well as other preserves so aim to use it within 6–8 weeks. I prefer to store it in the fridge at all times.

Makes about 400g (1 jar) | Preparation time: 10 minutes | Cook time:10 minutes

Lemon and Lime Curd

2 large eggs

1 egg yolk

225g caster sugar

Finely grated zest and juice of
  1 large lemon

Finely grated zest and juice of
  2 limes

50g unsalted butter

1. Beat the eggs, yolk, sugar and citrus juices together then strain into a heatproof basin that will sit easily in the pressure cooker. Stir in the citrus zests. Put flakes of unsalted butter over the surface.

2. Cover the bowl with a double thickness of baking parchment, twisting and folding under the rim to secure. Place in the steamer basket in the pressure cooker. Add 250ml water to the pan with the citrus shells (instead of lemon juice to help prevent discolouration of the pan).

3. Cover with the lid and bring up to High pressure, then reduce the heat and cook for 10 minutes.

4. Remove from the heat and allow the pressure to reduce slowly at room temperature.

5. Lift the bowl out of the cooker with the help of the basket. Remove the greaseproof and stir gently. Pot in clean, warm jars, cool, label and store in the fridge.

This is delicious with any cold meats or cheese but particularly with cold turkey, duck or chicken. Alternatively, try it with wedges of Camembert, dipped in egg and breadcrumbs then quickly fried until golden – the perfect starter served on a bed of rocket.

Makes about 1.2 kg (3 jars) | Preparation time: 15 minutes | Cooking time: 12 minutes

Spiced Apple and Cranberry Chutney

2 large onions, chopped

1.35kg cooking, or windfall eating apples, peeled, cored and chopped

100g dried cranberries

100g sultanas

500ml cider vinegar

½ tsp cayenne

½ tsp ground ginger

1 tsp mixed spice

1 large garlic clove, crushed

1 tsp salt

300g soft light brown sugar

Lemon juice (optional)

1. Put the onions, apples, dried fruit, vinegar and spices in the pressure cooker.

2. Cover with the lid and bring up to High pressure, then reduce the heat and cook for 8 minutes.

3. Remove from the heat and reduce the pressure quickly under cold water.

4. Add the remaining ingredients and stir well. Bring to the boil in the open cooker and cook, stirring frequently, for about 4 minutes until thick enough to softly plop off the spoon in a dollop, and not runny or too stiff. Taste and sharpen with lemon juice if using sweet apples.

5. Pot in clean, warm jars, cool, label and store in a cool dark place. Once opened, store in the fridge and eat within a few weeks.

The nice thing about chutneys is you can vary the flavours according to whatever ingredients you have in abundance: apples, pears, plums, even runner beans or marrows. Experiment – as long as you get the sweet/sour/spicy flavour, you'll have a winner!

Makes about 1.2kg (3 jars) | Preparation time: 15 minutes | Cooking time: 15 minutes

Pear, Date and Walnut Chutney

1.2 kg unripe pears, peeled, cored and chopped

200g chopped dried dates

100g walnuts, roughly chopped

2 star anise

1 cinnamon stick

1 dried chipotle chilli

500ml distilled white vinegar

1 tsp salt

2 tsp tamarind paste

300g soft light brown sugar

1. Put the pears, dates, walnuts, spices and half the vinegar in the pressure cooker.

2. Cover with the lid and bring up to High pressure, then reduce the heat and cook for 8 minutes.

3. Remove from the heat and reduce the pressure quickly under cold water.

4. Add the remaining vinegar with the salt, tamarind and sugar and stir well.

5. Bring to the boil in the open cooker and boil, stirring frequently, for about 7 minutes until thick enough to softly plop off the spoon in a dollop, and not runny or too stiff.

6. Discard the spices. Pot in clean, warm jars, cool, label and store in a cool dark place. Once opened store in the fridge and eat within a few weeks.

If you grow courgettes and a few grow too big, use them instead of marrow in this easy-to-make chutney. You could use butternut squash as an alternative too. You can use malt vinegar and 1 tbsp pickling spice tied in muslin instead of the ready-flavoured vinegar if you prefer.

Makes about 1.8kg (4 jars) | Preparation time: 10 minutes | Cooking time: 13 minutes

Marrow and Ginger Chutney

1.4kg marrow, peeled, deseeded and diced

2–3 tbsp salt

2 onions, chopped

1 large cooking apple, peeled, cored and diced

225g sultanas

1 tsp ground ginger

600ml pickling vinegar

5cm piece cinnamon stick

100g soft light brown sugar

1. Put the marrow in a colander and sprinkle liberally with salt. Stand it in a shallow bowl and leave overnight to remove excess moisture.

2. Rinse the marrow thoroughly, then place in the pressure cooker with the onions, apple, sultanas, ginger and half the vinegar.

3. Cover with the lid and bring up to High pressure, then cook for 8 minutes.

4. Remove from the heat and reduce the pressure quickly under cold water.

5. Stir in the remaining vinegar, the cinnamon and sugar. Bring to the boil and simmer in the open cooker for about 5 minutes until thick enough to softly plop off the spoon in a dollop, and not too runny or too stiff.

6. Discard the cinnamon stick. Pot in clean, warm jars, cool, label and store in a cool dark place. Once opened store in the fridge and eat within a few weeks.

This full-of-flavour sauce is a delicious condiment with meat, fish or poultry and great with chips! You can also use it to enrich pasta and other tomato sauces or to spread on pizza bases before adding toppings. Store in the fridge and, once opened, use within two weeks.

Makes about 600ml (1 bottle) | Preparation time: 10 minutes | Cooking time: 8 minutes

Fresh Tomato Sauce

1.8kg ripe tomatoes, roughly chopped

150ml red wine vinegar

½ tsp ground ginger

½ tsp ground cloves

¼ tsp grated nutmeg

A large pinch of chilli powder

175g soft light brown sugar

½ tsp dried basil

Salt and freshly ground black pepper

1. Put the tomatoes in the pressure cooker with the vinegar.

2. Cover with the lid and bring up to High pressure, then cook for 3 minutes.

3. Remove from the heat and allow the pressure to reduce slowly at room temperature.

4. Transfer the mixture to a blender or food processor and rinse out the pressure cooker. Purée the sauce, then rub through a fine sieve and return to the pressure cooker.

5. Add the remaining ingredients, stir, bring to the boil in the open cooker and simmer for about 5 minutes, stirring frequently until thick enough to softly plop off the spoon in a dollop. Pour through a funnel into a sterilised sealable bottle, leave to cool, label then store in the fridge.

Index